GOOD DIRT

Lent, Holy Week & Eastertide

A Devotional for the Spiritual Formation of Families

Lacy Finn Borgo & Ben Barczi

This book is dedicated to the Good Dirt Families community,
whose stories and experiences
of raising children in the Kingdom
inspire us daily.

The Daniels, Texas
The Liebenthals, South Korea
The Morykons, South Carolina
The Ouedraogos, Togo
The Quinns, Colorado
The Rundels, Michigan
The Tylers, New York
The Weyels, California
The Youngs, Colorado

Read their insights at www.gooddirtfamilies.com

CONTENTS

. . . .

Appendices

SERIES INTRODUCTION

Dirt Matters

Pete Collum is my (Lacy's) grandfather and at his very core he is a gardener. Wherever he has lived, he has planted something. When he and my grandmother, Lillian, lived in a dilapidated building that used to be their deli grocery store, surrounded by machine shops and oil field workers, he found tiny patches of dirt and planted watermelons, tomatoes and okra. Armed with a hat that had seen better days, a pocket full of seeds, and a belief in the miracle of growth he stepped into the realm of the Creator and worked. That Permian Basin dirt is full of shale and black gold, but it needs a bit of help if you hope to get squash and tomatoes. He is always puttering around outside, burring scraps, propping up plants, watering, irrigating, and weeding.

It has been said that nature is the first book we read about God. As created beings on a created planet we learn so much from simply looking around a bit.

As a little girl sitting on a paint can in PaPete's garden, I watched him. I saw how the presence of water can change even the look of a plant in a matter of minutes. I saw that if you pull weeds when they are small, their roots are smaller so require less elbow grease to remove. I saw that the row where we buried garden scraps months before had the healthiest plants. I tasted warm watermelon still on the vine, sweetened by the sun.

While listening to Dallas Willard at the Renovaré Institute for Spiritual Formation, this scene came back to me. Spiritual formation has remarkable similarities to garden living and tending. Of course, as parents of young persons and children of God, we live in the garden we tend. The metaphor of the garden can help us enter spiritual formation more fully. And, since we are seasonal creatures born on a seasonal planet, it made perfect sense to me to engage in the Seasons of the Church as part of family spiritual formation. Knowing right away I was in over my head, I enlisted a fellow student, Ben Barczi, for help. He's a spiritual formation pastor who lives the Seasons of the Church. We brainstormed this idea and wrote *Good Dirt* together. It is our desire that our voices are heard in harmony and so many of the narratives are written in first person.

Spiritual Formation: Tending Your Garden

God has given us both the seed of our own souls and the souls of the little ones that live in our homes and leave their gum on the table. Our job is to till, plant, water, and weed, doing what we can to make our family soil rich in the love of God. In the same way that gardens need constant care, so do souls, both little and big ones. This devotional is designed to help you work in the garden of your family throughout your day. It is designed to help you set a daily rhythm of tilling, planting, watering and weeding.

» **Till:** Greet the day with prayer, such as, "Good Morning Master Gardener. We will need your help today. And thanks for the rain." Perhaps praying together at the breakfast table will work for your family, or snuggled together in bed before the day begins.

» **Plant:** Meditate on scripture, for the good seed of God is his Word. There is nothing better for the little and big souls in families. Read it aloud. Have your newest family reader read, or your oldest, or boldest. What an honor to speak these words of life. If everyone is willing, read it twice. Read it slow. Let it seep in—let it leach the life-giving vitamins and minerals into the family. Let it feed these souls.

» **Water:** Reflect. We've got to have water. Water not only hydrates, it also carries vitamins and minerals to where they are needed. Reflection, like water, is a carrier: it carries the truths of scripture straight to the center of the heart where they can do the most good.

» **Weed:** Examine. If weeds are not pulled in a garden they will choke out all life. That is the harsh truth of gardens and people. Even pre-schoolers can examine their days. They know very well when they have obeyed and when they have not. Just before bedtime is the perfect time to examine the day, to ask the questions: what in my day today was life giving, and what was not? How did I walk in the light today, or not? Ending with prayer entrusts the process of growth into God's hands:

> *Lord, we brings these things to you. Glory to Father and to the Son and to the Holy Spirit, as it was in the beginning, is now, and will be forever, Amen.*

Suggested Rhythms for Daily Garden Care:

» **Rhythm #1:**
AM (Breakfast): Till and Plant
Noon: Water
PM (Dinner): Plant and Water
Bedtime: Weed

» **Rhythm #2:**
AM (Breakfast) Till
Noon: Plant
PM (Dinner): Plant, Water
Bedtime: Weed

» **Rhythm #3:**
AM (Breakfast): Till
Noon: Plant, Water
PM (Dinner): Plant, Water
Bedtime: Weed

» **Rhythm #4**
AM (Breakfast): Till, Plant
Noon: Take a pause to thank the Giver of Growth.
PM (Dinner): Plant, Water
Bedtime: Weed

There are many different combinations that can be used for daily garden care. Between waking up and going to bed, just be sure to till, plant, water, and weed, as a family. As flexible as this can be, it is very helpful to establish a rhythm, the same time to do the same thing day after day. Daily rhythms evoke a sense of security. Rhythms give families a knowing expectation of what is to come.

Spiritual formation has four major elements: your life, spiritual disciplines, Jesus' life, and the Holy Spirit. We have woven these elements into the daily and monthly rhythms. The first element of spiritual formation is **your life.** As a smart-mouthed teen of the '80s I often quipped at friends, "Get a Life." But the truth of the matter is we have a life. We may not love it, and it may not be exactly what we wish, but I've got a life, and you've got a life. You've got a garden. In your garden there is rain, sleet, drought, squirrels, and perhaps on some days too much manure. In your garden you have sprouts; the tiny plants God has given you, the ones that look to you for food and water. The tiny plants that beg to stay up past their bed time, the ones that argue with their sister. The ones that beg for candy in the checkout line, and give away their toys to a friend who has little. You have the shade trees of a good friends, or supportive family. Maybe you've even got a plant or two that would do better in another garden, but you keep it because it's just too hard to change and love rightly. And to keep it real, you've also got weeds; maybe they are sins that seek to choke you or your sprouts.

We are formed by our environment, for good or bad. I spent some of my earliest and best years in my grandparents' old deli in the middle of oil field workers and welding shops. I was formed by this environment. As a result, I learned hospitality: my grandparents welcomed each person who entered their deli. Race or gender had no bearing on how they treated people. I learned responsibility; they gave me jobs to do and the value that came from them depending on my job. I also picked up a colorful vocabulary. I didn't know "shit" was not universally accepted vocabulary until I began attending a Christian School. I did learn fast though.

The second element for spiritual formation is **spiritual practices or disciplines**. These are tools that work life and light into our gardens. Some tools we have used before. They are tried and true. For example, I grew up in a Southern Baptist church, and Southern Baptists read their Bibles and journal. These are good tools to connect us with the Life Changer.

Sometimes we need to change out even our favorite tools. After a while, journaling became a place for me to judge others and whine about my life. So I took a good ten years off journaling. Only recently have I started again, and this time, I only write what I hear God saying to me. The old tool needed retooling, but throw a good tool away? Never. But if the ground has changed, or your soul has had more rain, or even drought, that may call for a new tool.

Spiritual disciplines or practices open the space for God to feed and shape your garden. For example, praying puts you in contact with the Master Gardener. Confession is an exercise in weed pulling. Simplicity keeps us from planting more than our soil can sustain. These habits form us. In this devotional we will engage in many of these life-forming habits. We will practice twelve classic practices Richard Foster writes about in his book *Celebration of Discipline*, as well as some others.

The third element for spiritual formation in families is **Jesus' life**. Dallas Willard describes the work of spiritual formation as taking on, bit by bit, Jesus' ideas and images about God, life, and the world, so that they gradually replace our own. We want to be able to look at our everyday life—the dishes, the noisy neighbor, the grubby kids, the mailman, our boss—and be able to see them and live with them in light of the loving, good God that Jesus knew.

The primary place we get instruction and guidance on the with-God life is Jesus. "No one has seen the Father," Jesus' best friend, John, wrote. Now there's a problem—how can we do life with someone no one has ever seen? But John knew the solution, because he snuggled up to him at the Last Supper: "This one-of-a-kind God-Expression, who exists at the very heart of the Father, has made him plain as day." (John 1:18, *The Message*)

It is in the one-of-a-kind life and teaching of Jesus that we get the help we need to replace our unhelpful images of God and life with the ones that shaped the mind of Jesus. We watch him talk to God, rejoice in God, weep with God, listen to God, and lead others to God. And, most of all, we see him show God's love: eating with sinners, touching the untouchables, and laying down his life with arms stretched out to embrace the world. That's why in *Good Dirt* we journey with Jesus through the Gospels. In the recorded memories of the disciples, the research of Luke, the reminiscing of Peter handed to Mark, we have an expression of the life of Jesus that takes our breath away—if we will pay attention!

So we need to meditate on and study Jesus' life. Both of those terms get a bad rap, because they sound either mystical or boring. But kids do both naturally. Meditation is just turning over and over an idea, imaginatively, entering it and playing with it and seeing what it means and how it works. Kids meditate on ladybugs and anthills and dogs' tails and sand between their fingers. And study—far from being boring work done in a hushed library—is keeping our attention on something so that it becomes part of us. Kids study their favorite super hero, they study mom and dad, they study cartoons and they study their older siblings. ("He's copying me!" Yes, exactly—the child is watching and absorbing mannerisms until they think and act just like the one they've studied.) So studying and meditating aren't as much of a stretch as we'd think, and the Gospels make wonderful material to study Jesus and his one-of-a-kind God-Expression life.

We also get help in journeying with Jesus from the Seasons of the Church. In this devotional we are immersing our lives in the life of Jesus by celebrating the Seasons of the Church. Another way to say it is that we are marking our lives by the life of Jesus. The Christian Church began formally celebrating Easter as early as 325AD, and even before that Israel had seasons of fasting and feasting to mark their story with God throughout the ages. There is a great cloud of witnesses that have gone before us.

The seasons follow a pattern of preparation, celebration, and then living out what we have prepared for and celebrated. In Advent we prepare for God with us, at Christmastide we celebrate God with us, and during Epiphany we step into a life with God. In Lent we prepare for our own death and the death of Jesus, at Eastertide we celebrate that he died, is risen and us with him, and during Pentecost and Kingdomtide we live out his resurrection and ours. We are meant to live seasonally. Who can feast all the time without becoming a glutton? Who can fast or mourn all the time without losing their mind? When our days lose the gift of thankfulness and celebration we become a depressed and dying people. As the physical seasons set the rhythm of the earth, so the church season can set our rhythm to the rhythm of Christ.

There are seven main seasons of the church. The great diversity of our Christian traditions means that some seasons are named slightly differently and some dates are variable, but this is the overall, middle of the road, happy medium, church calendar.

Seasons of the Church

» **Advent:** Four weeks. Color: Royal Blue

» **Christmastide:** Twelve days, until the eve of Epiphany on January 5. Color: White

» **Epiphany:** Eight weeks, give or take a few weeks depending on when Easter falls; plus a little at the beginning and a little at the end to get us to Ash Wednesday for Lent. Color: Green

» **Lent:** Five weeks, plus a little at the beginning and a full week of Holy Week. Color: Purple

» **Eastertide:** Seven weeks up to Pentecost Sunday. Color: White

» **Pentecost:** One week, which is included as the last week of Eastertide. Color: Red

» **Kingdomtide:** Twenty-eight weeks, give or take a few weeks depending on when Easter falls. Color: Green

Do all these dates sound confusing? No worries, we put a calendar of specific dates at the end of the book. In time these seasons will become second nature.

How to Make a Seasons of the Church Calendar

First, a confession. The first three times I made one of these it was a disaster, mostly because I'm an adult. In my first attempt, I couldn't make myself label the seasons counter-clockwise. The calendar moves counterclockwise to remind us that we live countercultural to the world and its systems of destruction and death. However, in my forty years on this planet, I have learned that everything moves clockwise; going against the grain requires more thinking than I can summon. Funny thing though, my seven-year-old and ten-year-old pulled it off. "It's easy, Mom," they said. Likely story. In my second attempt, I spelled Epiphany wrong, in permanent marker. My Southern Baptist roots betray me. Who ever heard of Epiphany in the first place? And for my final attempt, I couldn't get the dashes evenly spaced to mark the weeks. There were rulers, protractors, and a host of other instruments I hadn't used since high school geometry. Once again counseled by people not even of driving age, I realized I was letting this calendar use me. Got it. So I stepped back and let the kids make it. It's great and it's attached to our fridge.

> **Materials:** poster board, pencils, permanent markers, rulers (only one and no more tools) crayons, 1 brass brad

> 1. This calendar will look very much like an analog clock. Cut a large circle (as large as you want your calendar to be) out of the poster board.

> 2. Divide the calendar into seven sections, like a pie graph. Take a look at the seasons listed above, estimate that, for example, Kingdomtide will need the most space because it has the most weeks. Pentecost and Christmastide will have tiny spaces. Remember: the seasons go in counter-clockwise order. For example: make a space for Advent, then move to the left for Christmastide, etc. If you get stuck ask your kid for help.

> 3. Within each season make "dashes," like the five minute marks on an analog clock, to represent the weeks contained in each season.

> 4. Write the name of the season on its space. Fill in the season space with its color (see the list above).

> 5. Cut out an arrow from the poster board. Use the brass brad to attach it to the middle of the calendar.

Optional Additions: Put a star on Christmastide, and a Cross on the first week of Eastertide. Invite or encourage your children to research the history and tradition of the seasons and write a list of their symbols in their space. Decorate the house with these symbols when their season comes around. A friend of mine has wind chimes hanging over her kitchen bar, and changes the items on the chime as the seasons change. We change the items on our mantle. All of this is not to make us consumers; in fact it's more fun to make some of these items. Like the icons used in the Orthodox Christian tradition, they are open windows into the life of Jesus. They remind us that we mark our lives by his life.

The fourth element for spiritual formation in families is the **Holy Spirit**. We can prepare the dirt, we can water and weed, but we don't make things grow. We have no control over sun, rain or wind. We aren't even in charge of the seed we are given: we do not choose our talents and inclinations. The Holy Spirit gives the seed. The Holy Spirit makes things grow. We do not control the outcomes, and it's a good thing: having control is dangerous for us. Getting just what we want and hope can make us hell to live around. Having complete control leads us to cast judgment on others. Even thinking we should have control can make us a mess. Think of the parents of children who have struggled or self-destructed? Parents who think they are in control beat themselves up for doing it wrong. They carry the crushing burdens of "should have", "would have" and "could have." How wonderful that we have the Holy Spirit working on our behalf. We learn to do our part and trust the Holy Spirit for the rest.

Everybody's Got Parts

In a garden, plants have parts. And those parts have different jobs and have different needs. People have parts too. The most obvious part we have is our body.

We were only one song into Sunday morning when Julie began to lead them in. All seven preschoolers followed dutifully behind our children's director to the front row. The switch to modern worship music hasn't been easy for most of the church. The hymns are the songs of their faith, their struggles, but graciously, they sing. They don't clap, but they do sing. And so did the preschoolers. They belted out those tunes like they had sung them all their lives. First they worshiped with their mouths. Then a few began to sway; they started clapping their hands; a few even let loose a full-body jig. As someone who is with children on a regular basis this was no surprise to me. I know they can't hide joy in their bodies. But I was surprised at how their transparency spread through the church. While the congregation watched the children, who frankly couldn't be ignored, folks began to smile, and then clap, and even—dare I say it?—sway. "Is this how the children will lead us?" I thought. They will lead us to worship God with our whole selves.

Children, like adults, have parts. Children have a body, a mind, a spirit, a soul, and a village. Dallas Willard in *Renovation of the Heart* calls "village" a social context.[1] This refers to the folks that influence us as well as the ones we influence. This village does shape us. Jesus mentions each of these parts as he gives us the For Dummies version of the Ten Commandments, "Love the Lord you God with all your heart [spirit], and with all your soul [soul] and with all your mind, [mind], with all your strength [body]..., and love your neighbor [village or social context] as yourself." (Mark 12:30-31) When we talk about spiritual formation we are talking about all these parts being invited into relationship with God. All of these parts come to live in the kingdom of God.

Our children's bodies which we lovingly wash and feed are created by God and created like all their other parts to be in relationship with him. As a born Southern Baptist, who is currently Nazarene, but loves everything Catholic, I have to say that the best part of the twelve days of Christmastide is meditating on the Incarnation. God himself enters creation in a human body, a real human body. The Gnostics and the Church Fathers went round and round over this. Did Jesus have a real human body, you know, one that got the flu and threw up, one that had body odor, one that danced when he felt joy, one that wept when he felt sadness? Our Church Fathers fought the good fight to say that, yes, he had and still does have a real body. For us, the incarnation, Jesus in a real human body, means that our bodies are redeemable. God's intention for bodies is goodness. He declares it so in Genesis 1, and who am I to contradict that?

Children cannot hide the condition of their spirit, mind or emotion behind their bodies. Adults can, but children simply cannot pull it off. This is a major advantage for children as we think about how they live their lives with Jesus. When they are sad, sadness leaks out of their eyes; it is shown in their bodies. Adults, on the other hand, have been taught when these emotions are appropriate and when they are not, and we are often trained to deny even having these emotions.

Equally so, children can't hide their thoughts. During sharing time in thousands of elementary schools across America, children are sharing what they are thinking about. Mostly what they have to say is not even loosely related to the topic at hand, but it's on their mind and they have a desire to tell someone.

---

1 For a full and frankly fantastic teaching on the parts of the person and how they are formed into Christlikeness check out *Renovation of the Heart* by Dallas Willard.

The desire to share comes from the divinely inspired, very human, desire to be known—for the hidden parts of us to be known and accepted by another. Children in healthy environments have no inclination that hidden parts should stay hidden or that any thought they have wouldn't be welcomed by any hearers.

Rightly ordered the spirit is the command center of the person. "Out of the heart the mouth speaks," the scriptures remind us. Jesus refers to it in his simple version of the commandments. "Love the Lord your God with all your heart and soul." However our spirit is formed so goes the rest of the person. Interestingly enough educational sciences are discovering that we are formed by experiences more than we are formed by formal teaching. Churches over the last hundred or so years have invested truck loads of resources in education of children and I think if we look back we might question the results. At least in the last twenty years we have seen a mass exit of young people from the church. Could one of the reasons be that formal teaching does not actually hold the weight in formation that experience does? Could it be that the experiences of formation offered by the secular world outweighed the formal teaching of Christian education?

The key to the power in experience over formal teaching lies in our wiring. We are created to take in information through our five senses, engaging all the parts of our person. What the body experiences is taken into the spirit, and like capillary action moves to all our other parts and formation happens. Living a life with God is not confined to an intellectual understanding. All the parts of the person live a life with God. Everything. He came to redeem it all. That's the good news. We get a whole, not partial, salvation.

Seasonal Fun

The seasonal fun section contains opportunities to mark our lives by the life of Jesus. In this section there are many activities, crafts, celebrations, suggestions, songs, harebrained ideas, and general chances for fun. Please, do not set out to do them all. Do not. You will make yourself and your family crazy. Instead, during each season choose a few, the ones that are suited to where you are in your family, for example toddlers versus teenagers. Next year choose some that you didn't do the previous year.

Marking your life by the life of Jesus for one year will change you for sure, but imagine with me the difference it will make marking it each year for the rest of your life on earth. Imagine. Imagine the difference it will make in the lives of your children as you bring them into the knowledge and relationship with Jesus first through observation and participation in the rituals of the season and then when they are old enough reading through the gospels.

Seasonal Fun is where we live out in our bodies the marking of our lives by Jesus' life. For example, the celebration of Eastertide has its chance to work resurrection into our minds through bodies as we have a mini-celebration every Sunday during the seven weeks of the season.

Family Structures

In this devotional we reference moms and dads and children. But rest assured, if your family structure doesn't look like this, this is still for you! Today's family structures are varied and those structures too are included in Jesus' invitation to the kingdom. Our intimate communities often include friends, and extended family members. From my point of view this is wonderful. When we use the word "family" in this devotional we are including those in your intimate community, those living and eating with you.

Family Listening

As a people we're pretty good about talking, and telling. We've got stories to tell and opinions to convey. However, part of the relationship process with each other and with God is listening. In this devotional we will encourage you to practice listening. Good listening, complete with eye contact, affirmations, and a zippered lip. Every day you will be challenged to listen to God, and to discern with one another his voice and message. We often think of hearing from God as an other-worldly, only-when-smoke-is-involved matter, but that couldn't be farther from the truth. Listening to God, like listening to others, is a product of experience. You know your mother's voice because you have heard it over and over again. When we hear a voice we think is God's we check it against 1 Corinthians 13. Was the voice patient and kind? How about gentle and generous? If so that was God and we fix that experience in our souls. Each additional experience we have with God's voice builds our confidence. After a while it won't be long before we don't even have to look we know it was God who spoke, because we've heard him before.[2]

And What about the Littlest People?

This is a family rhythm, and because families can range in ages, we've aimed at the middle. Every aspect—Till, Plant, Water and Weed—can be "rounded" up or down. "Rounding" up is rarely a problem, but what about the littlest members of our family? How does this nurture the preschool people?

These little interactive sponges have all senses on go! The real value of ritual, which involves so many of the senses, is spent on the little ones. Each night during Advent as the candles are lit, their minds are drinking in that 'light dispels darkness' and 'the One who is celebrated is the light.' The regularity of ritual teaches far more than wordy explanations. The Seasonal Fun section is the main teaching tool for small children. In living the seasons and reading the scriptures year after year, an essential foundation is being built on the Rock. They are listening when the scriptures are being read. Furthermore, they understand far more than we realize. It is not that we, the knowing adults, have to introduce them to God. They very recently were knitted together in their mother's womb. They know the Knitter. However, at their developmental stage they lack the language to express what they know. It is, nevertheless, up to us, their parents, to teach them the language, and to teach them what a relationship with God looks like on this earth.

---

2 Dallas Willard's book *Hearing God: Developing a Conversational Relationship with God,* has been instrumental in deepening our knowledge and practice of hearing and discerning the voice of God.

LENT

. . . .

Lent is the season of the divine paradox: we must die to live. Nature echoes this paradox. Seeds must die to live. Stars die to birth galaxies. It is the way of creation, and we are created. While the other seasons of the church burst with life, Lent brings us firmly to our deaths. As we observe Jesus' walk toward his cross, we become aware of our own. As he said, we must die to live.

Using our gardening metaphor, Lent is weed-pulling and tree-pruning. It is the decay of composted materials that will eventually enrich our soul soil. My (Lacy) gardening is a comedy of errors, except there's not much laughing. Two springs ago I decided I needed a strawberry garden. I hauled over goat manure to mix into the soil before planting my tiny new plants, some fifty of them. I painstakingly designed my watering system and dreamed of the mouth-watering delights that would soon be my reward.

Boy, was I wrong. The little plants did grow, but so did the hidden enemy: the not-so-decomposed alfalfa seed in the manure. My Mom always said manure was nothing but grass and water; now I knew she was right. Since the manure wasn't fully composted, along with my precious strawberry plants I inadvertently planted alfalfa. Somewhat digested alfalfa, but alfalfa nonetheless.

In an alfalfa field, alfalfa is good; in a strawberry garden, bad. I spent the remainder of the spring and summer and fall and until blessed winter came pulling weeds. Everybody got a chance to pull weeds. Children, grandparents, visitors all took a turn in the strawberry garden. One hot summer afternoon I was pulling in this garden, which is flanked by an old St. Francis statue that has been repainted by various children who seem to have gained their painting skills from the circus. I desperately wanted to burn the whole patch down, with fire or chemical. All this work for a few delights that I could buy from the grocery store didn't seem worth the effort. I stared at St. Francis, giving him the stink eye, like all of this was his fault. He smiled his usual smile and continued to hold out the bread and wine.

I persistently pulled those weeds while my mind drifted to spiritual practices. The efforts that make our spirits strong and healthy are often like weed pulling. Confession, fasting, simplicity, submission are just a few that came to mind that afternoon. Eventually I began a routine of confession each time I stepped into that weedy holy ground. This confession was a conversation with God in which I could tell the truth about myself and tell the truth about God.

This is Lent.

Practicing Lent with Children

It seems Christmastide and Advent, with all their indulgences, are seasons custom-made for children, but what about Lent? What do we do with children and death? Aren't we to teach them to live? Herein lies the paradox. It is our job to teach them to live, but they must also learn to die to themselves in order to really live. They must learn to die to having their own way, and they must learn to give away what they have in order to receive what God has for them. If we live in a constant state of indulgence we will never live a whole life. When we deny ourselves, die to our wants and needs, wholeness seeps into us and we live. Lent is our salvation from the superfluous.

One of the "weeding" spiritual practices is submission. The discipline of submission is the act of willingly giving up having to have our own way. Submission is never to be forced; the power to choose must always reside in the person doing the submitting. Forced submission, like slavery, will break the soul and is a horror. Conversely, chosen submission is a beautiful thing. Jesus freely gave his life for us. It was not forced on him; he chose it. Nelson Mandela's Truth and Reconciliation Commission showed us that freely given mutual submission heals nations and peoples.

Like submission, confession, sacrifice, and fasting are all Lenten practices that are not to be forced, but chosen. We can invite our children to practice this "weeding" by choosing it ourselves. Our children will watch us choose, and it is my experience that they will follow. We teach them to die, by dying ourselves.

Not so long ago I (Lacy) was at my Grandfather's house, helping take care of him in his last days, which were only a few. I remembered my Aunt Nita on her death bed, saying that she didn't know how to die because she had never done it before. I watched my Grandfather struggle with the same thing. How do we go about dying? When does our innate striving for life cease so that we can let the wholeness found in death come to us? To learn this we may look to Jesus, who not only taught us how to die by dying on the cross, but died to having his selfish way every day of his life. He practiced dying daily. He made a way for it.

We can also make a way for death. We can clear the path, clean the space, and set our houses in order. That is what we do during Lent as we participate in the three disciplines of **prayer**, **fasting** and **giving**. Together these disciplines do in us what we cannot do for ourselves. They clear the path, clean the space and set our spiritual houses in order so that God can bring death to our self-absorption, and replace it with blessed glorious resurrection.

With all this death talk we may think we must spend Lent walking around with sour looks on our faces. Not us, the people of God! In Lent the paradox kicks in, and we are joyful. It's the kind of joy that knows Love is on its side. Our joy is not the superficial pleasure of indulgence; instead it's sturdy. It's the sturdy love of Jesus' mother Mary and Mary Magdalene at the foot of the cross. It's the sturdy love of the Good Samaritan, and of our Good God who forgives over and over. Love makes Lent joyful. What we do, we do out of love for God and for neighbor. As a family we struggle together, drawing us into one another, and there is joy in that.

Can't you see it? The Kingdom of God stands on its head in defiance of a world that says, "Get all you can and share with no one." When we say "no" to our wants, we can say "yes" to the needs of others. Lent is our chance to collectively say, "We give all we can and share with those in need." In Lent we discover that self-denial makes our families richer instead of poorer.

Lent is forty days long, plus Sundays. It begins on Ash Wednesday and ends during Holy Week. Why forty? Those forty days have roots in the forty days of Noah on the ark, the forty years of Israel in the desert, Jonah's forty days of penance for Nineveh, and for Jesus' forty days of fasting in the desert. The color for Lent is purple, a color for the penitent.

The Big Three Lenten Practices: Prayer, Fasting and Giving

Three practices have, over the centuries, become central to the season of Lent. They work together to help us weed the garden of our hearts: prayer, fasting and giving. Throughout this season in *Good Dirt* we are exploring these practices in ways that families can enter together.

Since Lent is a penitent season it is important to remember and to tell our children that God doesn't need us to do these things or require us to do them. Doing these practices will not make us more loved or more worthy. God loves us just the same. We need to do these things in order to become the kind of people we want to be, people like Jesus. We are in need, not God.

One warning: Don't try to do everything. Pick a few practices and be consistent.

Prayer begins in the spirit. (For a reminder of the parts of the person, check out the Series Introduction under "Everybody's Got Parts.")

» Family Altar or Prayer Corner: Cover a small table with a purple cloth. Arrange on it a cross, or a family Bible; maybe a small, shallow, box with sand in it, where children can draw their prayers to God, or perhaps a family prayer journal. Choose a Christ candle to place in the center. (Battery powered candles are wonderful to use with small children.) Invite children to "light" the Christ candle in the morning or evening, or when you are reading the Bible as a reminder the Jesus is the Light of the World. This is the light of Advent that continued through Christmastide and Epiphany—and it still shines in Lent. Invite family members to visit the Altar at least once a day.

» Prayer Box: Take 3x5 index cards and write prayers on them from the Bible, or from saints, or beautiful pieces of poetry. (*This Is What I Pray Today* is a delightful prayer book for children written by Phyllis Tickle. Also *Prayers for Each and Every Day* by Sophie Piper has been a favorite in our home.) Place the cards in a box. Read one prayer each evening before bed, or at the dinner table.

Fasting begins in our bodies.

Fasting is not popular in our culture. Denying myself something I want will sound strange to others, but it is eminently important that we and our children learn to tell our bodies "no." Letting our bodies and their desires run our lives will destroy us.

Fasting is directly related to prayer. In fasting we teach our wills to ignore our mere desires and focus on our true needs. But the will is loud, and irritating, and is in the habit of responding to the body's wants. We need strength beyond our own to die to our desires and retrain our wills. Only the peace of God can quiet the will long enough for it to learn.

» Fasting from meat: Traditionally many folks fast from meat on Fridays, or whole forty days. If this works for you and your people, go for it.

» Fasting from superfluous food: Some I know have fasted from eating out for forty days; others have fasted from sugar, chocolate, or soda.

» Fasting from technology. For children, giving up nutritional food is not an option, but giving up TV, video games, or texting is.

Giving begins with others.

Giving begins right where we are. We look to our families and see where we take instead of give. We make the effort to overcome our natural pet peeves. We do something nice for someone who irritates us.

» Giving money: We choose to eat simple meals, or to fast from junk food, and give the money we save to someone else. There are many great organizations that truly give life to others.

» Giving time: We fast from our favorite TV show and give the time we save to packing the family up and visiting the local nursing home.

» Giving attention: We give up always having to talk about ourselves and give the gift of listening.

Family Fun for Lent

» Make a Poster of the Big Three: After you choose, as a family, which practice or practices you would like to do, put them on the poster as a reminder.

» Bury the Alleluia Banner: If you still have your Alleluia banner up from Epiphany or your Epiphany stars, now is the time to put them away. We bury our banner so we can dig it up again at Easter. Invite your children to hide it somewhere in the house.

» Plant a Seed: Take a clear cup and plant a seed next to the side, so that you can see the seed grow roots and change. Invite children to draw a picture of it daily, as it changes. Encourage them to do the watering. Remind them that we also change as we are watered with prayer, fasting, and giving.

» Order a Butterfly Kit: Carolina Biological Supply Company[3] has butterfly kits. If you have the means to do so, order one. Invite all the family members to observe the stages of change; when the butterfly emerges create a special ceremony for releasing.

» Sabbath: Many traditions honor a reprieve from fasting on the Sabbath, whenever it is observed. For many Christians this is Sunday, and the idea is that there should be nothing but feasting on the day that our Lord was raised from the dead. Not all traditions break their fasts on the Sabbath; either can be beneficial. You can do what your local church does, or have a family discussion and decision. What is not beneficial is to focus on breaking the fast, so that when the Sabbath arrives we indulge the obsession we've been ignoring. If we "save up" all our desires for one day, our bodies push our wills into gluttony, lust, and greed. In short, we become worse off than when we started. Eating a box of Twinkies on the Sabbath because we are fasting from dessert the rest of the week is not celebration, but gluttony.

» Saint Patrick's Day (March 17): Take a break from purple and color everything green. Here are a few suggestions for St. Patrick celebratory fun that doesn't include alcohol. (Sorry, parents.) Purchase a children's

---

3 Visit http://www.carolina.com to order.

book about St. Patrick and read it. Make a poster of the shamrock, and write Father, Son and Holy Spirit, one on each leaf. Play Celtic music and learn (or pretend) to dance a jig.

About the Readings

During Lent we are going to read straight through the first twelve chapters of the book of John. In such a somber period, John's gospel is full of light—the light of the glory of Jesus. More than any other gospel, John bursts with poetry and praise. His writing is crammed with excitement as he helps us see Jesus as the Son of God. But he also doesn't shy away from the darkness. Early on, John tells us that the darkness doesn't want anything to do with the light and flees from it so it won't be exposed. In Lent, we remember the darkness as we approach Jesus' crucifixion.

As we read John together during this season, it is a good time to ask ourselves questions, such as "What keeps us from drawing close to Jesus?" and "Where do we prefer to keep to our own way?" It's also a good time, amidst all the "tough stuff," to pause and celebrate that Jesus is God's answer to all of our fears and weaknesses. The Kingdom of God is here, in our midst—because Jesus is in our midst! "Behold, the Lamb of God, who takes away the sins of the world!"

Traditionally, churches do not use the word "Alleluia" during Lent. Reading John grows in our hearts a pent-up exuberance so that when Easter comes, "Alleluia" bursts from our lips!

WEEK OF ASH WEDNESDAY

Seasonal Fun:

On Ash Wednesday we remember that dust is where we began and dust is where we will return. Again, it is against our cultural norms to reject the perpetual quest for eternal youth. Ash Wednesday is a day to take a good honest look at ourselves, and confess how we have moved away from God.

» Practice confession. There is something powerful in naming our sins. Saying them out loud helps us to own them. And even more powerful is to hear the pronouncement of forgiveness spoken aloud. Often when we struggle to embrace the forgiveness of God, an oral pronouncement from a trusted friend or clergyperson will be all the help we need. We can also teach our children to look back as far as they can into their lives and think where they have not obeyed God, or where they have hurt someone else, building a holy habit of humility and grace.

» Prepare for Ash Wednesday by gathering as a family and spring cleaning the house. This is an outward symbol of our inward preparation. Everyone helps! From top to bottom and all accessory buildings: clean, clean, clean. Collect goods that are not used or needed or don't fit and cart them over to the Salvation Army, Goodwill, or some other charitable organization.

» Many churches hold special services for Ash Wednesday in the morning or evening. During a traditional Ash Wednesday service, ashes are applied to believers' foreheads as a symbol of repentance. If your church does this, ask how your younger children can participate. If your church does not offer such a service, consider visiting another that does.

Ash Wednesday

Till: God, you made us, and you know: we're made from dust, we return to dust. Thank you for being compassionate to us in our weakness, and accepting us in Jesus.

Plant: Luke 18:9-14

Water:

>> Play it: Encourage children to act out the parable Jesus tells in today's reading. This will help them visualize what Jesus is teaching.

>> Enter it: In this story, there are two men: one whose prayer focuses on his own goodness, and one who just asks God for forgiveness. Jesus says that the second man, who asked for mercy, was made right with God, and not the other. Why do you think that is?

>> Apply it: God forgives us when we confess our sins. (Read 1 John 1:9). What would it look like today if you trusted God and admitted when you are wrong, instead of hiding mistakes?

Weed: Lead your family in a time of confession at the end of the day. Where did you fall short of loving God and loving others? Be sure to thank God for his forgiveness. Then reflect: What was it like today, admitting mistakes instead of hiding them? How was it hard? How did it change your attitude?

Thursday

Till: Jesus, you are the Lamb of God—you take all our sins away! Your cousin John recognized you immediately. Help us to recognize you today.

Plant: John 1:29-34

Water:

» Play it: In today's reading, John the Baptizer points out Jesus as the one who gives forgiveness. Invite the children to act out the scene where John recognizes Jesus then baptizes him. Use your imagination to see what the Holy Spirit would look like falling on Jesus. John says the Holy Spirit looked like a dove; what do you think?

» Watch it: John the Baptizer was looking for Jesus. He knew Jesus was the one who was forgiving people. Today, watch for people who are forgiving others. How can you be like Jesus and forgive others?

Weed: When did you see people being forgiven? When did you forgive others? What made you feel good today?

Friday

Till: Jesus, we want to see what life with you is really like. Thank you for inviting us to be your students. Help us get rid of anything that keeps us from following you.

Plant: John 1:35-42

Water:

» Enter it: In today's reading, Jesus invites some disciples to "come and see" what life with him is like. We learn to be like Jesus by being with him. Name some things you have learned how to do by being with your mom or dad. How did it feel to learn from them?

» Apply it: What are some things that keep you from wanting to learn from Jesus? How can you stay with Him today? (A wonderful young man, who was merely four years old, remembered to turn his thoughts back to Jesus every time he burped. Try that!)

Weed: When did you "come and see" with Jesus today? Did you learn anything from him today? What did you enjoy today?

Saturday

Till: Jesus, your invitation is open for everyone—come and see! Help us to be your students, and to invite others to learn from you, too.

Plant: John 1:43-51

Water:

» Create it: Draw a picture or make a Silly Putty sculpture based on today's reading.

» Apply it: In this story, Philip, one of Jesus' students, invites Nathanael to join in and "see for himself" what Jesus is like. What is something you are learning from Jesus? Is there anyone you could invite to learn that from Him, too? How could you invite people to learn from Jesus today?

Weed: What did you learn from Jesus today? When did you share what you learned? What made you feel good today?

LENT, WEEK 1

. . . .

Sunday

. . . .

Till: Jesus, you are with us and it's a time to celebrate. Help us learn that you are better than anything we give up.

Plant: Mark 2:18-22

Water:

» Enter it: In this passage, Jesus talks about fasting—giving up food or something else in order to focus on God. While he was here, his disciples didn't fast because it was a celebration! What would it be like if you went to a birthday party, but refused to eat cake and acted really sad? How would the birthday person feel about that?

» Apply it: Talk about what you have chosen to give up during this season of Lent. How can your fast (or your cravings or habits) remind you to look for Jesus today? (Or, if you are taking Sundays off of the fast, how can enjoying this thing today remind you to rejoice in Jesus?)

Weed: How did your fast help you look for Jesus today? (Or, if you are taking Sundays off of the fast, how did today remind you to rejoice in Jesus?)

Monday

Till: Jesus, you take ordinary things and make them extraordinary! Help us be faithful in our daily lives, and trust you to make them beautiful.

Plant: John 2:1-12

Water:

» Play it: Have children act out this story. This can be especially fun if you have the child playing Jesus drop in some red food coloring into a pitcher of water and mix it. (Just be sure to explain that Jesus didn't really need to add food coloring!)

» Enter it: Water is ordinary, but wine is for celebrations. What is one ordinary way you obey God? (Maybe it's helping your parents with the dinner dishes? Maybe it's making your bed? Maybe it's doing your homework?) Ask Jesus to make that ordinary something into something wonderful.

Weed: What ordinary way did you obey God today? Where did you see God's extraordinary work? Celebrate that by thanking God!

Tuesday

Till: Jesus, clean out of our lives everything that keeps us from you! You love us so much. You want what is best for us. Do whatever it takes, Jesus!

Plant: John 2:13-22

Water:

» Play it: This scene could be very fun to act, but use your judgment on how riled up you're willing to let your kids get. One calmer game would be to scatter toys, Legos, stuffed animals, and coins around the floor of a room and have kids sweep them up with a broom.

» Apply it: Jesus was passionate about letting nothing get in the way of knowing God! The people were distracted with money and things. Are there things in your life that sometimes distract you from God? How could you return your attention to him today?

Weed: When were you able to return your attention to God today? Tell about a time you were distracted today. How can you invite him into that time tomorrow?

Wednesday
. . . .

Till: God, we need you—on our own, we're not so good at life. We don't know how to follow you, or how to love others. Please come and give us a whole new kind of life so we can really live, in you.

Plant: John 2:23–3:15

Water:

» Enter it: This is a long and tricky passage, but one thing is clear: Jesus is teaching us that life with God isn't something we can do by ourselves. Life with God is something God gives, sometimes in ways we don't understand. We need his help. What are some ways you need God's help?

» Apply it: Tell about a time when you saw a living thing—plant or animal—being born.

Weed: How did you ask God to help you today? How did it feel asking for his help? What happened? When were you happy today?

Thursday

Till: God, you love us so much, you're willing to forgive everything we do wrong. You sent your Son to show us just how much you love us. Help us to accept your love and not hide from you today.

Plant: John 3:16-21

Water:

> » Draw it: Create a picture of this verse: "God-light streamed into the world, but men and women everywhere ran for the darkness." (John 3:19, *The Message*) When do you hide from God's love and truth?

> » Apply it: Jesus is showing us what God is like. God wants to forgive everything, and put the world right! How does this passage make you feel about God? About Jesus?

Weed: How did God's love help you today? When did you feel like hiding from God today? Why?

Friday

Till: Jesus, you are greater than anyone else! You deserve all our love and attention and obedience. Help us to point to you, instead of making a big deal about ourselves.

Plant: John 3:22-36

Water:

> » Apply it: In this passage, John the Baptizer shares that he is perfectly willing to give up the spotlight so that people can know Jesus. He isn't attached to people's praise; he doesn't need to be the center of attention. Think of someone else about whom you could make a big deal today—someone that you could encourage, or do something for, and

make them feel special. Who can you serve today? And how? Make a plan.

» Visit the Altar: Read a prayer card, or draw a prayer in the sand.

Weed: What made you happy today? How did it feel to make a big deal about someone else? How did it feel to see them feel special and loved? How can you practice being a servant tomorrow?

Saturday

Till: God, we are thirsty for your love. Sometimes we try to quench our thirst in ways that leave us thirsty. Forgive us, and help us thirst just for you, because you will fill us up!

Plant: John 4:1-26

Water:

» Draw it: Draw the scene of Jesus talking with the woman at the well. What is the expression on Jesus' face? How does he feel about this woman?

» Enter it: Jesus is teaching that he is like a well of water that is always fresh, always refreshing. But we try to drink from stagnant, murky pools and aren't satisfied. This woman was trying to satisfy her thirst through her many marriages. Can you think of some ways you try to satisfy your thirst apart from Jesus?

» Apply it: How is your Lenten fast affecting you? Is it helping you turn toward Jesus more?

Weed: What did you enjoy today? Today, when did you feel "thirsty?" Were you able to bring this to Jesus?

LENT, WEEK 2

....

Sunday

. . . .

Till: Jesus, we are all ears. We are listening to you! Help us to listen even more to you. Help us obey, so we can be students who learn to be just like our teacher. Help us to be like you.

Plant: Mark 3:31–4:9

Water:

> » Draw it: Create a picture of the plants in each of the four soils: the hard road, the gravel, the weeds, and the good earth. Which of these plants is most like you?

> » Apply it: Jesus tells us that the people who are his students are as close to him as family. How does it make you feel to know you're in God's family? What is one way you could act like Jesus' family today?

Weed: Tell about a happy or sad thing that happened today. When did you have an opportunity to act like Jesus' family today? Remember that you are a precious child of God and nothing can change that.

Monday

Till: Father, your way is real food that keeps us filled up. Help us to enjoy the plenty that comes with obeying you!

Plant: John 4:27-42

Water:

> » Enter it: Jesus knows where real life is found, and he says that for him, obeying his Father is like eating a scrumptious meal. How does it make you feel when you know you have pleased your parents?

> » Act it: Assign parts, inviting the family to act this scene out.

Weed: Was there a time today that you felt God smile at you? How did it feel? How is your fast making you feel about yourself? How is it making you feel about God?

Tuesday

Till: Jesus, heal us! We bring you our worries, our bad habits, our sickness and sadness. It's life or death for us, but if you just say the word, we will be healed! You are in control.

Plant: John 4:43-54

Water:

> » Imagine it: How do you think the father felt when he discovered his son was healed? How do you think his family felt when they found out that Jesus had healed the son?

> » Sculpt it: Think about that one thing you need God's help with today. Sculpt that thing. Leave it on your family altar and pray, "Jesus, I need your help with this."

Weed: How did Jesus help you today? Was it easy or hard to trust Jesus with hard things? Why?

Wednesday

Till: Jesus, we act like you when we show love to others and care for them. It's more important to show love than to follow the rules. Help us to see how we can love people around us.

Plant: John 5:1-18

Water:

> » Play it: Invite children to act out this scene. Invite someone to play Jesus, the crippled man, and the Pharisees who respond angrily.

> » Apply it: In today's story, Jesus healed a crippled man, but some people got mad because they were worried about keeping rules. They missed the joy of a miracle because it didn't fit into their rule book! Jesus loves others. What is one way you can love others today?

Weed: Tell about a way you loved others today. Tell about a time someone loved you.

Thursday

Till: God, you have opened the door to us. We can talk with you and be with you as much as we want. You have put Jesus in charge, and he shows us how to do it. Help us wake up to you today.

Plant: John 5:19-29

Water:

> » Play it: Play a game of Follow the Leader. Be sure everyone gets to take a turn being the leader. Afterward gather everyone together and tell how Jesus and God love each other so much they follow each other's lead. They may take turns being the leader, but they always follow each other.

> » Spot him: Where do you think you might spot God today? (When you see or show love, joy, peace, patience or kindness, you spot the work of God.)

Weed: When did you feel happy today? When did you spot God or his work today?

Friday

......

Till: Jesus, you amaze us: even though you are equal with your Father, you don't push ahead without him. You are happy to trust your Father, and wait for him. Help us, also, to trust our Father and trust you.

Plant: John 5:30-47

Water:

> » Enter it: Jesus says that, even though he is God's Son, and has all power, he never does anything on his own. Instead, he listens patiently and works with his Father. Is that surprising to you? How do people in charge normally act?

> » Apply it: Where is one area where you could practice listening to God and obeying him today?

Weed: When did you listen for God today? How did it feel? When is it hard to listen for God?

Saturday

Till: Father, forgive us—sometimes we hide from you because we don't like being corrected when we're wrong. Help us have courage to admit when we're wrong and stay close to you.

Plant: John 7:1-13

Water:

> » Enter it: Jesus says that the world is "up in arms" against him, because he exposes its evil. Why do you think people don't like admitting they are wrong?

> » Apply it: Confession is an important way to stay close to God. Confession means to tell the truth about ourselves. So we admit to God we have done what he calls wrong and that we need forgiveness. Today, take some time to write a note to God, telling the truth about yourself, perhaps laying it on the Family Altar.

Weed: How did it feel to take time for confession? How does it feel to know God forgives you?

Read 1 John 1:9 (we read it earlier during Lent, but it's a good reminder). Before going to bed, offer each other a blessing, reminder each other that we are forgiven. (For example, lay a hand on your child's shoulder or head, look her or him in the eye and say, "In Jesus Christ, you are forgiven, and you are God's beloved child. Amen.")

LENT, WEEK 3

· ·

Sunday

· · · · · · ·

Till: Jesus, you are powerful! You can defeat any evil, and drive away any enemy that would harm us. We are amazed by you!

Plant: Mark 5:1-20

Water:

» Draw it: Make a drawing of part of this story that captures your imagination. Share your drawing and tell why you chose this part of the story.

» Apply it: Jesus shows that he has power even over a rioting mob of evil spirits. Where do you need to see that Jesus is powerful today?

Weed: Did you see Jesus' power today? Where? Describe what you saw. Invite Jesus' power to stay with you and protect you tonight.

Monday

Till: Jesus, you take what little we have and turn it into a miracle of plenty! Small things make a big difference in your hands. Use our small lives in big ways today, for your kingdom!

Plant: John 6:1-15

Water:

>> Play it: Have children act out this story. What are the expressions on the disciple's faces as Jesus multiplies the bread and fish?

>> Enter it: How do you think the disciples felt about Jesus when they saw this miracle? How do you feel about him?

Weed: When were you surprised by God today? Did he do something you didn't expect? Tell about a time when you didn't feel like you could do something, but God helped you through it.

Tuesday

Till: Jesus, what you provide lasts forever. Give us what we need today, and help us be content with what we receive from you.

Plant: John 6:16-27

Water:

>> Create it: Draw a picture or create a Silly Putty sculpture of Jesus walking on the water by his disciples' boat.

>> Apply it: In yesterday's and today's readings, Jesus shows that he is powerful. Then he makes the promise that he can meet all our needs. We don't need to worry; instead we can get close to him and trust him to provide. Where can you trust Jesus to help and provide today?

Weed: What made you happy today? How did Jesus provide for you today? Thank him for the ways he loves you!

Wednesday

Till: Jesus, we're joining you! There's nothing better for us than to live with you, trusting you. Help us to remember to join with you today.

Plant: John 6:27-40

Water:

» Imagine it: What would happen if you tried to sit on a tree limb that was too small? Or walk across a bridge that was too weak? Why do you think it is safe to put all the weight of our lives on Jesus?

» Apply it: Practice putting your weight on Jesus today. Whenever you feel overwhelmed, or frustrated, imagine that all the burdens you feel are resting squarely on Jesus' shoulders, and you're safe in his arms. How can you remember to do this all day long?

Weed: When did you throw your weight on Jesus' shoulders? How did it feel? Did you forget, or try to shoulder the weight alone? How did that feel?

Thursday

Till: Jesus, you are the bread of life. Your presence and power nourish us and sustain us each day. Always give us this bread. Always give us yourself!

Plant: John 6:41-51

Water:

» Create it: If you have time (or a bread machine), bake a loaf of bread and set it aside. Put it on your Family Altar as a reminder that Jesus is the bread of life! (Later on, when it gets stale, you could use it to go feed birds or ducks at a park, and think of Jesus blessing his creation.) If time is short, you could have kids draw a picture, or just use a store-bought loaf of bread.

> » Apply it: During Lent we are giving up something that we usually hope will nourish or sustain us. How can your fasting today remind you that Jesus is the bread of life?

Weed: What did you enjoy today? What are you learning from your Lenten fast? When are you experiencing Jesus making up for the lack of the thing you've given up?

Friday
......

Till: Jesus, you broke your body and shed your blood so that we could live free from shame and free from sin. How can we thank you? Help us marvel at your mercy and love today.

Plant: John 6:52-59

Water:

> » Enter it: Today's reading points to our need for Jesus, but it also reminds us of the symbol Jesus gave us in Communion. Today, celebrate Communion with your family. Share the bread and say, "The body of Jesus for you." In the same way, pour juice for each family member and say, "The blood of Jesus for you." (If the children are too young, or in your tradition you take Communion only from an ordained minister, another option is to put the elements as the centerpiece at dinner and talk about what they mean.)

> » Visit the Altar: Read a prayer card or draw a prayer in the sand.

Weed: What does it mean to you that Jesus gave his body and blood to save you?

Saturday

Till: Lord Jesus, we admit that your teachings are hard for us to understand sometimes. They are hard to believe, hard to obey, hard to trust. Keep us from walking away; bring us to you! Let us see that you have real life.

Plant: John 6:60-71

Water:

> » Enter it: Jesus kept on saying things that made people upset, things that made them leave. Why do you think the crowds left? Why do you think his twelve disciples stayed with him?

> » Apply it: Sometimes what Jesus asks us to do or believe can be hard. What do you find hard to believe sometimes? When do you find it hard to obey?

Weed: When did you see goodness today? Where did you stay close to Jesus today? When did you want to leave him behind?

LENT, WEEK 4

. . . .

Sunday

. . . .

Till: Lord, help us! We are so quick to try to do life on our own, to think we know everything, and to miss what you are doing because we are focused on what we are doing. Please clear out our pride and help us rely on you!

Plant: Mark 8:11-21

Water:

» Create it: Today Jesus warns the disciples against the "contaminating yeast" of the Pharisees. To help kids understand this point, fill a clear glass with water, then put in just a drop or two of food coloring. Allow it to stand for a day, and observe what happens—all the water changes color!

» Apply it: The disciples don't seem to understand that they can rely on Jesus for every need! They are in the boat, squabbling about bread, when he's just miraculously divided bread for thousands of people! Are there times when you tend to forget to rely on God, and focus only on what you can do without him?

> » Live it: Today, take "pause" moments to invite God to provide for you throughout the day. A "pause" might be everytime you take a drink. Say a short "Thank you" to God.

Weed: When did you rely on God today? How did that feel? When did you try to do it on your own? How did that feel?

Monday
········

Till: Jesus, you came from your Father in heaven, and you went back to your Father in heaven, all to help us know God. Thank you for helping us to know God.

Plant: John 7:14-36

Water:

> » Draw it: Draw the scene between Jesus and the Pharisees and the crowd. How do you think each group feels?

> » Imagine it: Jesus says that he was sent by his Father, so he knows him. Jesus knows God better than anyone. How do you think Jesus feels about his Father? How does the Father feel about Jesus, his Son?

Weed: What made you happy or sad today? When did you notice God today? Where could you spend time with your Father tomorrow?

Tuesday
········

Till: Holy Spirit, we are thirsty! We long for joy, love, happiness, and they are only found in your presence. Come and quench our thirst today!

Plant: John 7:37-52

Water:

> » Enter it: Jesus is talking about thirst again. Do you remember when we talked about the woman at the well and how Jesus said he would give water so we would never thirst? What are some ways that you have "thirsted" over the past few weeks? What are things you've wanted, or hoped for?

> » Apply it: How has giving something up for Lent changed how you thirst for God?

> » Visit the Altar: Read a prayer card or draw a prayer in the sand.

Weed: Were you thirsty today? How can you take your thirst to God tomorrow?

Wednesday

Till: Jesus, you are our light! Show us the way to live, to love others, to love you. Light up our path!

Plant: John 8:12-20

Water:

> » Enter it: Light a candle to symbolize Jesus as your light (especially in a dark room, if you can). Or, give kids flashlights. Ask, "How is Jesus the light for your life?"

> » Apply it: What is one situation in which you need Jesus' light to show you how to live?

Weed: Where did you need Jesus' light today? Did you ask for it? Where do you need Jesus' light tomorrow?

Thursday

Till: Jesus, help us to live in the truth, so we can be free from the tangles we get caught in. Lies trap and tangle us, but your truth sets us free!

Plant: John 8:21-32

Water:

> » Enter it: Jesus says that the truth sets us free. Tell about a time when being dishonest got you trapped or caught. Tell about a time when telling the truth was scary, but you did it anyway,

> » Apply it: Jesus teaches us that we don't need to lie. We live in God's kingdom, and he will take care of us as we live in truth. Try an experiment of not twisting, bending, or concealing the truth today. (Though you don't need to say things that would hurt people!)

Weed: How was your truth experiment? When was it hard? When was it good? When do you find it the hardest to tell the truth?

Friday

Till: God, you are our Father. Help us to behave like your children. Help us today to honor you, love you, and work with you in our world.

Plant: John 8:33-47

Water:

> » Enter it: Jesus taught that when we're children of God, we learn to behave like our Father. Tell some of the ways that you are like your mom or dad. Any skills, or hobbies, or interests that you have learned from them?

> » Apply it: How could you be a child of your Father God today? What do you think he is up to in your world?

Weed: How were you a child of your Father today? How did you act like him? When did you forget that you were a child of God today?

Saturday

Till: Jesus, you are the beginning and the end. You were around long, long before the world was created. Everything that exists was made through you! We praise you, Jesus!

Plant: John 8:47-59

Water:

» Create it: Have kids create a timeline of any events they know from world history or Bible history. Don't worry too much about getting it right—just let it be a history brainstorm. Then, have them draw Jesus at every point, and then way before and way after.

» Apply it: How does it make you feel to know that Jesus has always existed, and always will?

Weed: What did you enjoy about today? When did you notice Jesus today?

LENT, WEEK 5

Sunday

Till: Jesus, your ways aren't our ways. We have such a hard time with self-sacrifice, serving, and letting go of things we want even when they aren't good for us. Help us to trust you more. Help us to release control and follow you, even in hard situations.

Plant: Mark 8:31–9:1

Water:

» Imagine it: When Jesus told his disciples that his path was leading to suffering and death, they couldn't believe it! Peter even told Jesus to stop being so gloomy! Why do you think they reacted that way? How do you think you would have reacted?

» Enter it: Jesus' way leads through suffering and loss. We have to follow him through it too so that we let go of the things that keep us from God. Tell about a time when you had to do something hard that you didn't like, but turned out to be good for you.

» Apply it: Is there an area in your life where you need to give control to Jesus? What is one small step you could take today?

Weed: What was hard today? How did you feel about it? What was easy today?

Monday
········

Till: Jesus, you are this world's light—open our eyes! We want to see you! We want to see the truth. Lead us, Jesus!

Plant: John 9:1-17

Water:

> » Draw it: Draw a scene from today's story.

> » Apply it: Jesus opens eyes. He can heal a blind man and he can help us see the world the right way. Where do you need freshly opened eyes to love God and people today?

Weed: When did you see differently today? What did you see differently? What made you happy today?

Tuesday
········

Till: Jesus, help us to really see what we see. Help us to accept what you show us, when you show up! Help us to see you and believe.

Plant: John 9:18-41

Water:

> » Enter it: Why do you think the Pharisees didn't want to believe in Jesus' miracle? Why does Jesus call them blind?

> » Apply it: Are there times you'd rather ignore God? Why?

»   Act it: Assign parts, and act out this scene.

Weed: Where did you see God today? Tell about a time when you ignored God today.

Wednesday
. . . .

Till: Jesus, you are the Good Shepherd! Help us to listen for your voice, and to recognize you when you call us.

Plant: John 10:1-18

Water:

»   Create it: Draw a picture or make a Silly Putty sculpture of Jesus the Good Shepherd with a sheep. Place the sculpture on the Family Altar.

»   Imagine it: Jesus says he is the Good Shepherd. A good shepherd will take care of his sheep—us! Jesus says his sheep know his voice. What do you think Jesus' voice might sound like? How can you listen for Him today? (Re-read the "Family Listening" section in the Series Introduction, page 12.)

Weed: When did Jesus speak to you today? What did He say?

Thursday
. . . .

Till: Jesus, you are God! What a wonderful, amazing truth. God in skin and bones, God with us! There is no one like you, Jesus! We worship you, our God and King!

Plant: John 10:19-42

Water:

> » Enter it: Jesus tells us that if we will just look at what he does, we'll see that he really is God! What are some things Jesus did that tell you he is more than just a good teacher?

> » Celebrate it: Worship Jesus, our God! Put on some worship music and dance, sing, play, and celebrate him!

> » Visit the Altar: Read a prayer card or draw a prayer in the sand.

Weed: When did you make a big deal about Jesus today? What do you love best about Jesus?

Friday
......

Till: Jesus, you are the Resurrection and the Life. Help us put our trust in you when it seems everything we love and hope for falls apart. Help us remember that you are still in control.

Plant: John 11:1-27

Water:

> » Enter it: How do you think Mary and Martha felt when they found out their brother died?

> » Apply it: This week's story is a foreshadowing of next Friday, Good Friday, when we'll remember Jesus' death on the cross. Because God can bring new life even in death, sometimes he allows us to experience sadness so he can create joy out of it. Tell about a time when you were very sad. What came out of that?

Weed: As we come near to the end of Lent, what have you learned from praying, giving, and fasting?

Saturday

Till: It's a miracle! Life out of death! Restored hopes and dreams! Jesus, with you, every hurt is transformed into a joy! Help us trust that you can turn every hurt into a joy.

Plant: John 11:28-44

Water:

> » Create it: Draw or paint the scene of Lazarus coming back to life. How do his friends and family feel?

> » Apply it: Jesus has power to turn the darkest situations into new and abundant life. Where is one area you need him to bring new hope? Ask Jesus for it now.

Weed: When did you ask Jesus for new hope today? How did it feel to turn to him in a hard situation?

HOLY WEEK

....

Holy Week begins on Palm Sunday and ends just as we launch into the celebration of Eastertide. Holy Week places the divine/cosmic paradox we observe during Lent—death to life—under the microscope. We take a good look, with our hearts and minds, at how Jesus himself lived this paradox.

As parents we may wonder how to explain the Christian mystery of death becoming life to our children. That is the blessing of ritual. The small rituals already set in place during Lent and in each additional activity for Holy Week have a miraculous ability to impart understanding to children. Year after year these rituals teach the paradox of death to life. Their theology will not be complex, but children will know that out of death comes life.

When children are young they relate best to the life part of the paradox. Spring is the breaking from the death of winter. Consistently pointing out all the signs of spring is a powerful reminder. Older children can understand and participate in the death to life paradox. Always bring discussions back to the fact: "Life wins." Older children can benefit and will mature from time spent practicing dying to their own wills, and in sincere, thoughtful meditation on the last week of Christ in which he moved from life to death, and back to life everlasting.

Palm Sunday

Seasonal Fun:

Holy Week is split into two parts. The first is Palm Sunday through Holy Wednesday, which does not take us into the suffering of Jesus; instead we look ahead to what is worth dying for. The first part is full of preparation and confirmation. As Joan Chittister says in her book *The Liturgical Year*, "These first days of Holy Week confirm: there are some things worth living for, even if we find ourselves having to die for them as well."

> » Welcome Home Party: Create a welcome banner for Jesus. Read the "Triumphal Entry" of Jesus (today's reading) as a family. Enjoy special snacks; even invite the neighbors to join you in welcoming Jesus home.

> » Create a Blessing Banner: Part of looking ahead from death to life is found in looking ahead from winter to spring. Use poster board and construction paper to make a flower garden. On each of the flower petals write a blessing or something worth living for. Use the poster as a Holy Week reminder that life triumphs over death.

Till: We thank you, Jesus, for showing us how to live a humble and good life. Help us today to prepare for your coming. Show us how to celebrate your arrival!

Plant: Matt. 21:1-16

Water:

> » Watch it: Watch for the love and life of Jesus today.

> » Visit the Altar: In the sand, draw a picture of your favorite thing about Jesus.

Weed: How did you celebrate today? How can you carry this celebration through to Good Friday?

Holy Monday

Seasonal Fun:

Holy Monday, Tuesday, and Wednesday are preparation days. These are the days to get out the good china, go to the grocery store, purchase the Easter Sunday clothes, plan the menu, buy Easter baskets. (Easter baskets are a typical American tradition, but, like new clothes, they are not necessary for an Easter celebration.) There will be little time for preparations once Thursday comes, so this is the time. Easter clothes were traditionally white to remind us of our baptism into our life with God. They don't need to be expensive or fancy to be set aside or deemed special.

» Invite the children to help wash the good china. Invite the whole family to plan the Easter menu. Little children can choose and create decorations.

» Make traditional Easter eggs and/or make Confetti Eggs. Poke a tiny hole in both ends of the egg, and then blow out the insides. Poke tiny confetti inside, with a note that says, "Jesus Lives." Take to church on Easter and spread the celebration.

Till: Hosanna! Blessed are you who comes in the name of the Lord. We worship you, Son of God. We want to worship you all day long!

Plant: John 12:9-19

Water:

» Draw it: Draw the procession of people celebrating Jesus!

» Apply it: When can you invite Jesus to enter into your life today?

Weed: When did you invite Jesus into your life today? When were you happy or sad?

Holy Tuesday

Till: Jesus, when it looks to us like our hopes are dead and buried, you are preparing to grow new life: overflowing abundance many times over! Help us to trust you.

Plant: John 12:20-26

Water:

> » Create it: As Easter draws close, spring is usually arriving with flowers! Have children gather some wildflowers or blossoms from trees and make a bouquet.

> » Continue with preparations for Easter (see Seasonal Fun on Holy Monday).

> » Visit the Altar: Draw a prayer about new life.

Weed: Where did you see God bringing joy today? What did you enjoy most about today?

Holy Wednesday

Till: God, you have made your name known and loved throughout all the world, because of Jesus! Help us to honor you today.

Plant: John 12:27-36

Water:

> » Draw it: Choose your favorite scene from today's reading and draw it.

> » Continue with preparations for Easter (see Seasonal Fun on Holy Monday).

Weed: How was God patient with you today? When were you patient with others?

Maundy Thursday

· ·

Seasonal Fun:

Maundy Thursday begins the second part of Holy Week, and with it comes a shift in focus. Its name comes from the Last Supper, when Jesus declares, "A new commandment (*mandatum*, in Latin) I give to you: love one another." At this point in Holy Week, we no longer prepare; we are instead immersed. We don't think to the future; we live in the present. We slow and quiet our lives and our homes so that we can focus on Jesus.

» Remove everything but the cross and the Christ candle from the Family Altar.

» Turn off the TV and keep it off until Sunday. If you can, do the same for computers and unnecessary phones.

» Read the account of the Last Supper together as a family.

» Begin dinner with the "highest ranking" family member washing everyone's hands. (You can do feet if you want; in our culture washing hands before dinner is customary.)

» Attend a Passover Seder meal; this is the traditional Jewish ritual meal that we believe Jesus was celebrating at the Last Supper. Ask around: there are often people in the community who like to include others.

Till: Jesus, thank you for your body and your blood that you gave for us. Help us to remember that when we eat and drink of you, we will never hunger or thirst again.

Plant: John 13:1-35

Water:

» Receive it: When did someone serve you today?

» Serve it: When could you serve another person today?

Weed: When did you share Jesus today through serving? When did you receive Jesus today by being served?

Good Friday

Seasonal Fun:

Good Friday is the saddest day of the church year. It is the day that hope dies. We are tempted to let our minds skip to Sunday, but we must resist. Easter can only be birthed from death. So we as a family sit in our sadness on this day. We lean into the pain and suffering of Jesus. On this day our faith is tried. Could we—would we follow Jesus to the cross? Is our love and devotion to him strong enough to walk with him through the valley of the shadow of death?

» Read the account of the crucifixion as a family (today's reading).

» Invite the family to wear black to signify mourning for the dead Christ.

» If your family doesn't normally make the sign of the cross, try it today. When we make the sign of the cross we give all of ourselves to God, we accept the salvation of the cross for all the parts of us, and we also remember that all parts of us must die in order to live. Using the tips of your fingers, begin by touching your forehead, then your chest. Touch the front of one shoulder and then the other. Make it slowly and carefully each time you pray today. As you make the sign think about Jesus' dying for the whole of us: our minds (forehead), our hearts (chest), and our bodies (shoulders). Explain the sign and his death to your children.

» At 3 P.M. today, blow out the Christ candle. This signfies Jesus' death.

Till: We can't say "thank you" enough for dying for us. Help us, Lord Jesus. Give us the strength, the love, and the devotion, to follow you wherever you may lead. We cannot do it by ourselves.

Plant: John 19:19-42

Water:

» Imagine it: What was the most difficult thing to imagine about today's reading?

» Share it: Which person do you most identify with?

Weed: When did you make the sign of the cross today? What did it mean to you? Where would be the most difficult place Jesus could lead you? How can you prepare to follow him anywhere?

Holy Saturday

We have no reading on Holy Saturday. It is a day where the silence of God is deafening. It's a day where we go ahead and give up—give up striving for more or better. The struggle to die to ourselves that we have practiced all through Lent, finally gets its death blow on this day. Here the paradox comes into full bloom: though we know Easter is coming, in the silence and solitude of a dead Christ hope is lost. Don't try to skate through Holy Saturday with distractions, or false hope. Avoid preparing for Easter celebration today. The only way to get to Easter (or resurrection) life is through this "dark night of the soul."

» Do not light the Christ candle today.

» Children, especially, will feel the sadness and emptiness of this day. They may even cry. Let them and cry with them. They may not be able to verbally express what they know to be true: their Jesus has died. They are sad, and so they mourn.

» Tell the children about how people were buried long ago. Tell them how Mary and Martha would have gathered up strips of cloth and herbs and oil to prepare Jesus' body to be buried. Gather a basket with strips of cloth (or let them unwind a roll of toilet paper), oil or perfume, and some herbs. Mary and Martha were not able to prepare the body of Jesus this day because of the Sabbath, but inviting children into the act of preparation helps them express grief.

» Use a baby doll, toilet paper, and a cardboard box. Invite the children to imagine that the doll is Jesus, then have them help you wrap the body and put it in the box.

EASTERTIDE

Easter is the day our lives are changed forever. Nothing, absolutely nothing will ever be the same. But for many of us Easter is as mundane as Tuesday's Twinkies. We put on clothes we hate, hunt eggs we will never eat, and yawn through the Easter service. It wasn't always this way. Easter is Christianity's oldest celebration. It began with the day Jesus rose from death, and the celebration hasn't stopped! Long before the church celebrated Christmas, we celebrated Easter. Easter should never play second fiddle to Christmas. We have Christmas because of Easter; Easter is the reason we celebrate Christmas. The Bread of Life conquered death—that's the best news there is!

As we've been journeying with Jesus this year, we have heard over and over again his teaching about the Kingdom of God. We've seen him claim to know God in a unique, one-of-a-kind way in the Gospel of John; we've watched as he heals and forgives and loves. And at Easter, we get the best news of all—this Kingdom life is the real deal! By overcoming death itself, Jesus proves that the with-God life simply cannot be held down! So as we set out to imitate his life, we can have confidence and joy that Jesus' abundant life truly is the best life on offer. From the drab, cold winter days of Lent to the dark sadness of Holy Saturday, the question is raised—how can any joy come out of such loss and sadness? Easter answers: God's power and life is so strong that it can go *through* death and come out victorious the other side!

The color of Eastertide is the same as for Christmastide: white, for the purity of Christ. Eastertide is a total celebration of life, and conveniently for us it occurs in the springtime, when life is bursting forth.

Ways to Celebrate the "Burstings"

» Find a farm you can visit to play with the baby animals. Talk with the children about God, the creator of life, and his goodness. Talk about the resurrection of the earth from winter's death.

» When you're in the car, or going from here to there, invite the children to help you look for signs of new life.

» Fill your house with flowers. Let the children water the flowers, and explain how they are participating in giving life to the flowers. Talk about the ways we can give life to living things.

Family Altar Suggestions for Eastertide

» Replace the purple cloth with a white one, the color of Eastertide.

» Light the Christ candle at your Easter Vigil or on Easter morning, and keep it lit whenever you are around.

» Add prayers for Eastertide to your prayer box. The book *Poems and Pryaers for Easter* by Sophia Piper is a good resource.

» Add wildflowers or an Easter Lily.

» Find your Alleluia Banner and hang it over the Altar.

Creating Celebrations

The Jewish calendar is loaded with celebrations. The Sabbath is weekly. Then there is Passover, Shavuot, Rosh Hashanah, Succoth, Simchat Torah, Hanukkah, Purim… and these are just a few of the major celebrations. Celebration is in our DNA, given to us through our Jewish heritage. With Christ we also received Easter, Christmas, Epiphany and others. As Tony Campolo likes to say, "The kingdom of God is truly a party."

Unfortunately, we forget. We forget that we are the inhabitants of the kingdom of God, and so we have a unique understanding of life. After living in Lent and through Holy Week, we know in our innermost parts that life comes from death, however absurd that may seem to others. We know that, contrary to all we're told by advertising, money won't make us happy. We know that loving our hateful neighbor is the only way to peace. We know that nothing can separate us from the love of God. We know that nothing can destroy us. We know that our lives are everlasting. That's not just good news, it's great news and a reason to celebrate!

Celebrations are wonderful bonding experiences. Tragedy draws us together, but celebration binds us. There is nothing like a good party to make a people one. God designed us that way. Why are there so many Jewish celebrations? God's people needed to bond together, their survival depended on their oneness before God. So they partied! For the early Christians, persecution was everywhere. They needed stability. They needed camaraderie. And every Sunday, they had a celebration.

What about us, families in the twenty-first century? Families are broken before our eyes. Our survival also depends on our oneness before God. We must bond together to make it: we need a party! Use the following suggestions to craft a weekly party. It doesn't have to be an all day affair (it could be over a meal), but at least once a week during Eastertide, celebrate.

To begin, read this meditation by A.W. Tozer aloud to the family. Then work through the Celebration suggestions and shape your own unique weekly celebration.

"Celebrating Our Oddness"
by A.W. Tozer

A real Christian is an odd number anyway.
He feels supreme love for one whom he has never seen.
He talks familiarly everyday to someone he cannot see,
Expects to go to heaven on the virtue of another,
Empties himself in order that he might be full,
Admits he is wrong so he can be declared right,
Goes down in order to get up.
He is strongest when he is weakest,
Richest when he is poorest,
And happiest when he feels worst.
He dies so he can live,

Forsakes in order to have,
Gives away so he can keep,
See the invisible,
Hears the inaudible,
And knows that which passeth knowledge.

Questions to Discuss:

»   What is special about your family? What makes you "odd?"

»   How has God been good to your family?

»   Is there a unique blessing God has given your family?

»   Based on your answers, give your weekly Celebration a name.

»   Choose one day a week. Maybe you already have a day that is special. It doesn't matter what day, but you must have one each week.

»   Break out the party hats and the good dishes.

»   Every family member attends.

»   No serious talk, only fun. Try things like dancing, or board games, sing songs (karaoke machines are hilarious—rent one), eat your favorite food.

»   Include a toast: Each week take turns on who gets to write (or, in the case of the younger ones, devise and dictate!) the toast and lead it. Start with the youngest member.

EASTERTIDE, WEEK 1

Easter Vigil

Consider starting your Easter party late Saturday night. If you have little people in your house, start as soon as it's dark outside. If your people are older start between 10 P.M. and midnight. (Warning: This will really wind your people up. If that's a problem for the peace and harmony in your house, try this again when you children are older.)

If your church doesn't hold an Easter Vigil service, find one that does and go at least once. Just to see what all the fuss is about.

If you can't find an Easter Vigil service in your area, try this at home with your family. Invite the neighbors! Go overboard! Take time with your family and plan your DIY Early Easter Celebration!

Materials you will need:

» Many bells—at least two for each person.

» A candle for each person, or a flashlight for the younger people.

» A set of music that sounds like celebration. That may be a worship CD, or Handel's Messiah. Or how about Kool and the Gang's 80's hit "Celebration"? Let your imagination run wild!

> » And don't forget the desserts: luxurious, rich, and loaded with fat and calories straight from God's good green earth. (If you are inviting friends, invite everyone to bring their favorite dessert.)

> » A Bible.

Order of Events:

(You don't need to follow this order exactly, but here is an idea of how an Easter Vigil can flow.)

Keep the lights off. Even as people arrive, don't turn on the light. Use a flashlight to help everyone get comfortable in your living room. Let the darkness settle in. Remember that we cannot appreciate light if we don't know dark. Keeping the lights off will initially make people uncomfortable, but they will settle in. Have one small light in order to read the Scriptures by.

> » Pray: Heavenly Father, you are good and you stick with us no matter what. Thank you for forgiving us. Thank you for continuously asking us to come back to you.

> » Read: Psalm 105, or Psalm 78, or Psalm 106

> » Sing: "Create in Me a Clean Heart"

> » Read: Matthew 26:47- 27:56

> » Sing: "Jesus Paid it All"

> » Read: Matthew 27:57- 28:10

> » Pray: Jesus you are the light of the world! You have brought life from death. Give us both your light and your life. Hallelujah!

Then, while lighting candles, turn on every light in the house, and ring bells! Be sure to light the Christ candle on your Family Altar.

> » Sing: "Joyful, Joyful we Adore Thee"

Let the party begin! Put on the dancing music, pour the wine, pass the desserts! Party until you can't anymore then head to bed with the Resurrection ringing in your heart.

Easter Sunday

Till: Hallelujah! You are risen, Jesus, you are risen, indeed! Nothing can stop you from giving us new life, because you triumphed over death. Hallelujah!

Plant: John 1:1-18

Water:

» Light it: Be sure to light the Christ candle.

» There are so many special things going on today that there probably won't be time to sit and have a usual activity time today. Instead, enter fully into the joy of Easter. Go party! He is risen, indeed!

Weed: What did it feel like to rejoice in Jesus' resurrection today? What made you happy today?

Easter Monday

Till: Jesus, help us to trust in God like you trusted in God. Teach us to work with you and not on our own. Remind us to ask you for what we need.

Plant: John 14:1-14

Water:

» Imagine it: What is the work that God is doing today? (Remember that anything truly good comes from God.)

» Apply it: How can you work with God in this today?

Weed: Where did you see God at work today? How did you work with God, or against God?

Easter Tuesday

Till: Thank you, Jesus, for never leaving us alone. Thank you for sending the Holy Spirit to speak to us, and to comfort us. Help us to open our eyes to your love. Help us not to miss the Holy Spirit.

Plant: John 14:15-31

Water:

> » List it: Make a list of the places you can see God's care for you. (In the sunrise, in the food you eat today, in a kind word spoken to you.)

> » Discuss it: In what ways can you see the Holy Spirit? How can we look for him? (Any time we comfort someone, the Holy Spirit is working in us.)

Weed: When did you see God's care for you today? When did you see the Holy Spirit today? Did he work in you? If so, how?

Easter Wednesday

Till: Oh God, help us to stay connected to you. Help us to talk and listen to you all day today. We want to know you more, we want to keep you in our minds and hearts. Help us.

Plant: John 15:1-15

Water:

> » Cut it: Show a house plant (ivy works well) to the children. Tell them that this plant is like our lives with God: We are one of the branches. If

we stay connected to the plant we get water from the plant and we get nutrients from the soil; we live by being connected. Now, cut off one of the branches. Ask the children what will happen to that branch. Let them tell you how it will die. Leave the branch on the table for the next day or so and encourage the children to compare the dead branch to the living plant.

» Discuss it: What are some ways you can stay connected to God today? Maybe take a leaf off the plant for each person to carry in their pocket throughout the day to remind them to continue talking with God and keeping connected.

Weed: In what ways did you stay connected to God? In what ways did you disconnect?

Easter Thursday
. . . .

Till: Thank you, God, for sending the Holy Spirit, the Spirit of truth. Help us to listen to him as he speaks to us today. Help us to ask him for the strength we need to stay connected to you.

Plant: John 15:16-27

Water:

» Rot it: Set an overripe banana in a plate on the kitchen table (for several weeks if necessary) and let the children watch it rot. Each day ask the children if they would rather eat a ripe fruit or this rotten one. Explain that the "food" Jesus gives us is ripe. It is good for us, and it tastes good as well. The "food" that the world gives us, (selfishness, and materialism) is rotten. Which one would you like? The trouble is people who don't know the Holy Spirit (the Spirit of Truth) don't know the difference, and they often eat the rotten fruit.

» Discuss it: This is a difficult reading for children and parents. The idea that our children will suffer for Christ is hard to swallow. Talk with your children about what it means to be rejected for Christ. Ask your children to share about a time they have been teased or treated badly because of their relationship with God. Share about a time you have been treated badly for the same reason. Encourage your children that they are not alone. Jesus was also treated badly. Many Christians in history were also treated badly. If your children are older, do a little research and read up on Christians who were persecuted for their faith. Read these stories together as a family.

Weed: Where did you see the good ripe fruit given to us by Jesus today? Did you "taste" it? Where did you see rotted fruit? Did you "taste" it?

Easter Friday

Till: Lord Jesus, help us to remember that whatever we go through, you have gone through it before. Remind us that you walk with us and we are never alone. Thank you for sending the Holy Spirit.

Plant: John 16:1-15

Water:

» Live it: If you have older children check out the "Kids of Courage" web site, by Voice of the Martyrs.[1] Seeing and reading about children who have given all they could and made the stand to follow Christ is an inspiration. In the western world, we are mostly insulated from these kinds of persecution. We may be thankful for the protection while we pray for our brothers and sisters who are suffering. Surf this web site with your children. Discuss the stories and pray with your children for the persecuted. Faith gives seed to faith.

» Visit the Altar: What does it look like to be with God? Draw that prayer in the sand.

Weed: In what ways does praying for those who are persecuted change how you see things? When were you happy or sad today?

---

1 Visit http://www.kidsofcourage.com

Easter Saturday

Till: Heavenly Father, we are so thankful that though sometimes we may be sad, we are never alone. You never leave us. You were with Jesus during the saddest part of his life, and you are with us during the saddest parts of our lives. Help us to bring our happiest times to you and our saddest.

Plant: John 16:16-33

Water:

>   »   Discuss it: Invite each family member to talk about the saddest time in their life. How did you know that God was with you?

>   »   Pray it: Who do you know that is having a sad time right now? Pray for that person to know that God is with them.

Weed: Did you see someone who was very sad today? How did you pray for them? How did you feel seeing someone who was so sad? What are some things you could say to show the love of God?

EASTERTIDE, WEEK 2

....

Sunday

·······

Till: Jesus, help us to live with God like you did. Help us to live like you lived with others. Teach us to live like you.

Plant: John 14:1-7

Water:

» Draw it: Take a piece of paper and draw a road across it. Reread John 14:6-7. Jesus said that he is the road to God. With his whole life he showed us how to live a life with God. Write down some of the ways Jesus showed us how to live a life with God on the road. (He listened to others. He obeyed God. He helped when he was needed. He forgave others. He loved others. He loved God. He talked and listened to God.) Save your paper; you will use it for the next three days.

» Think it: What are some ways you can walk this road today?

Weed: What did you enjoy today? What are some ways that you walked like Jesus today? What are some ways that you didn't walk like Jesus today?

Monday

Till: Jesus, thank you for showing us what God is like. Help us to walk with God like you do.

Plant: John 17:1-12

Water:

> » Draw it: Continue adding to your Jesus road from yesterday, using the Scripture passage from today.

> » Discuss it: What new thing did you learn about Jesus from his prayer?

Weed: What are some ways you walked like Jesus today? What are some ways you didn't walk like Jesus today?

Tuesday

Till: Thank you, God, for using Jesus to show us what you are really like. Help us to learn from him and walk with you.

Plant: John 17:13-19

Water:

> » Draw it: Continue adding to your Jesus road from Sunday using today's scripture.

> » Discuss it: What new thing did you learn about Jesus from his prayer?

Weed: What are some ways you walked like Jesus today? What are some ways you didn't walk like Jesus today?

Wednesday

Till: Oh Jesus, thank you for praying for us. Help us to become one heart and mind. Help us to learn to love each other just as you—Father, Son and Holy Spirit—love each other.

Plant: John 17:20-26

Water:

» Draw it: Continue adding to your Jesus road using today's scripture.

» Discuss it: What new thing did you learn about Jesus from his prayer?

» Visit the Altar: Draw a picture about Jesus in the sand.

Weed: What are some ways you walked like Jesus today? What are some ways you didn't walk like Jesus today?

Thursday

Till: Thank you, God, for sending John the Baptizer. Help us to change our ways in response to your good news.

Plant: Luke 3:1-14

Water:

» Proclaim it: The passage from Isaiah that Jesus quotes is great news! Invite everyone to read it aloud together with gusto. Or invite your most dramatic member to read it as a proclamation in a king's court.

» Act it: Assign parts and invite your family to read and act out verses 10-14.

» Discuss it: What is the best news you have ever heard? What did you do in response?

Weed: What made you happy today? How can you tell if your life is green and blossoming? What can you do to help your life)bloom, produce fruit, show forth new life…)?

Friday

Till: Help us, Father God, never to forget that we are not in charge. You are in charge. You are the one who can clean our heart house. You are the one who will put everything in its proper place.

Plant: Luke 3:15-22

Water:

>   » Think it: What in your heart house needs to be cleaned? How can you connect with the Holy Spirit so he can clean your house? If we ask, the Holy Spirit will tell us what parts of us are dirty, or full of sin. Then we can repent of (or turn away from) those sins.

>   » Plan it: When today will you make time to confess, that is, to tell the truth about ourselves?

Weed: What made you happy or sad today? Do you need to say you are sorry for something you said or did? Do that now.

Saturday

Till: Jesus, help us to be full of the Holy Spirit so that we also can refuse the tricks of the Devil.

Plant: Luke 4:1-13

Water:

» Act it: Read the passage again aloud, inviting family members to act it out.

» Discuss it: In what ways is the Devil tempting you? Make a plan to get away from him.

Weed: How were you tempted today? How did you respond? What can you do to keep from falling to that temptation in the future?

EASTERTIDE. WEEK 3

....

Sunday

. . . .

Till: Lord Jesus, we love you. Help us to love you with our actions. Remind us today that we show love to you when we love others. Let us see someone we can love today.

Plant: John 21:15-25

Water:

> » Do it: We often say we love people, but how do we make that true? Actions. Saying we love someone is only half of love; doing acts of love makes love whole. What are some ways you can show love today to those you say you love?

> » Discuss it: Talk about popular movies and how they show love. We love someone if we want what is best for them. How is this kind of love different from the "romantic" love that is often shown in the movies? How can we know if someone really loves us? (They want what is best for us.)

Weed: Who did you see that needed love today? What did you do? Did you see people talking about love that wasn't really love today? What did you think?

Monday

Till: Make us humble, Jesus. Help us to know that we are broken and need you to fix us. Help us when we think we are whole, even though we are not.

Plant: Luke 4:14-30

Water:

> » Learn it: Read 1 Kings 17, then discuss the differences between the widow and the people in Luke 4:28-30 who had heard Jesus speaking in the synagogue. Which one are you most like?

> » Apply it: We can only depend on Jesus if we know we need him. If we think we are perfect, we then will think we need no one. Where do you struggle with thinking you don't need him, or that you are enough? Where do you need Jesus today?

> » Visit the Altar: Draw your prayer to Jesus in the sand.

Weed: What made you happy or sad today? Who did you see today that reminded you of the widow? Who did you see today that reminded you of those who heard Jesus in the synagogue? Who were you today? Where did you struggle today? Where did Jesus help you?

Tuesday

Till: Remind us, Jesus, of your power today. Help us never to forget that it was you who called the heavens into being. You are part of the Trinity. You have ultimate power, and you are the Son of God.

Plant: Luke 4:31-37

Water:

> » Imagine it: Reread the passage, slowly and deliberately. Quiet your mind and imagine that you are in the story. Which person are you? What does the Holy Spirit have to say to you through this?

» Process it: Jesus has all the power God does. How does that make you feel? How do you think it made the people in the story feel? Knowing this, how will today look different from yesterday?

» Create it: Make a banner that tells about the power of Jesus. Hang it in your house.

Weed: When did you see people today who reminded you of this story? If so, who and how? How did your day seem different, now that you know that the Jesus you talk with has all the power of God? Did it change anything? Did it change you?

Wednesday

Till: Jesus, your news is the best news. You brought God's kingdom to us right here, right now. We are so thankful. Help us to share that kingdom, and its good news, with others.

Plant: Luke 4:38-44

Water:

» Act it: Act out the scene in the today's story.

» Discuss it: Jesus makes broken people whole. Isn't that great news? In what ways are you broken? Where do you need Jesus to make you whole?

» Pray it: Can you think of some broken situations? Pray together as a family for Jesus to make them whole.

Weed: What made you sad today? Where did you see broken people or broken situations today? How did you pray? What can else can you do? How can Jesus use you to bring wholeness? Pray as family for the brokenness you saw today.

Thursday

Till: Oh Lord, you know more than we do! Often we think we know better or know more. Help us, Jesus, to remember that you are the smartest man who ever lived. And because you still live, no one can know more than you.

Plant: Luke 5:1-11

Water:

» Act it: Act out the story, after assigning the adults parts as fish. Laugh.

» Discuss it: What problem do you have today that you don't have a solution to? Pray with your family and ask Jesus to give you the best solution. Then, when you encounter a problem during the day, ask the smartest man who ever lived for a solution.

Weed: What problems did you have today? When did you ask Jesus to help you? What happened?

Friday

Till: Jesus, you amaze us! We've never seen anything like what you do! You heal us from broken bodies and broken souls. Help us look for your miracles today, big and small.

Plant: Luke 5:12-26

Water:

» Act it: Act out the verses 12-16.

» Sculpt it: Use Silly Putty and sculpt the scene in verses 17-26.

» Plan it: Plan a skit based on verses 17-26 that uses a large refrigerator box as a prop—drop by your local appliance store and get one—then make acting it out the entertainment at your Celebration this week.

Weed: Jesus can heal the body and he can heal us from sin. What are some sins you struggled with today? Pray with your family, asking Jesus to heal you from them.

Saturday

Till: Jesus, your coming is the greatest reason for celebration ever! You are the best partier, because you invite everyone to participate. Help us to party like you.

Plant: Luke 5:27-39

Water:

» Plan it: Make this week's party the best. Imagine it is Jesus' party. Hang festive decorations, play fun music, rent a karaoke machine. Invite people who you don't know very well. Invite people you wouldn't normally invite. Make the best, most elaborate food you can. Throw it like he's showing up because he might! Rejoice, the Kingdom of God is a party!

» Visit the Altar: Add something to the Family Altar that reminds you to celebrate.

Weed: What made you happy today? What was it like to plan and enjoy such a party?

EASTERTIDE, WEEK 4

. . . .

Sunday
. . . .

Till: Jesus, you are the sure and stable rock on which we can build our lives! Help us to be wise and to trust our way to you, so that when storms come we are safe in your care.

Plant: Matthew 7:15-29

Water:

» Sing it: "The Wise Man Built His House Upon the Rock"[2]

The wise man built his house upon the rock,
The wise man built his house upon the rock,
The wise man built his house upon the rock,
And the rains came tumbling down!

The rains came down and the floods came up,
The rains came down and the floods came up,
The rains came down and the floods came up,
And the house on the rock stood firm.

---

2 If you're not familiar with the tune, a quick search on YouTube turns up several versions!

The foolish man built his house upon the sand,
The foolish man built his house upon the sand,
The foolish man built his house upon the sand,
And the rains came tumbling down!

The rains came down and the floods came up,
The rains came down and the floods came up,
The rains came down and the floods came up,
And the house on the sand went SPLAT!

» Build it: Build houses, using blocks or Legos; with older children you can use playing cards. Help the children build, while talking about how important it is to build a strong foundation. Show them how a house on a shaky foundation will fall down. Talk about how God is a strong foundation. When we talk with him and live our life with him, we build our lives on the rock.

Weed: What made you happy or sad today? What does a life built on a strong foundation look like? What does a life built on a weak one look like? How do you know the difference?

Monday
. . . .

Till: Jesus, we are so happy that you are in charge! You are always doing good and helping people; teach us to do the same.

Plant: Luke 6:1-11

Water:

» Discuss it: Jesus said he was Lord of the Sabbath: not a slave, but in charge. Sometimes when we pray, we think that God has to do what we ask, like he is a slave. Here Jesus reminds us that he is in charge. He knows what is good, and what will really help people. We can ask and trust that God knows best.

» Pray it: Talk about a need someone has. Then have one or two minutes of silence to ask God what he wants for that person. Then listen to God's answer. (Remember that God always wants what is good and he wants to help people.) Then pray, asking for what God wants.

Weed: When did you pray today? Did you ask God what he wanted? Did what you wanted and what God wanted ever differ?

Tuesday
. . . .

Till: Jesus your words are full of life. Your words feed us and make us whole. Help us to eat your words today.

Plant: Luke 6:12-26

Water:

» Preach it: Using verses 20 through 26 or so, invite anyone who wants to do so to preach this section. Give everyone a chance.

» Listen to it: Which part of these verses did the Holy Spirit bring to your attention?

Weed: The people mentioned in these verses are people who are not blessed in our world, but Jesus is saying that they are blessed because God's kingdom of good news belongs to them too! Who did you see today who is not blessed in our world? Did you remember that they are blessed in God's kingdom?

Wednesday
. . . .

Till: Jesus, you loved your enemies. Teach us to love our enemies. Teach us to pray for those that hurt us. Help us to trust that you can take care of us.

Plant: Luke 6:27-38

Water:

>» Discuss it: Tell about a time someone hurt you. Jesus says that we are to love our enemies. If we love someone, we want the best for them and we do the best for them. Sometimes the best for someone is to not let them do evil again. Sometimes the best for someone is to serve them. How can you love the person who hurt you?

>» Pray it: Pray with your family about how to love those who hurt us.

>» Visit the Altar: Draw a prayer in the sand about a time someone hurt you. Invite Jesus to heal you.

Weed: Did someone hurt you today? How were you able to pray for them? Can you think of someone who thinks of you as an enemy? How can you make that person your friend?

Thursday

Till: Jesus, you know the way. Guide us! We need you to lead us every day.

Plant: Luke 6:39-49

Water:

>» Play it: Use items in your house to make an obstacle course. Use a tea towel to blindfold one member of your family. Invite another person to guide the "blind" one through the obstacle course. Discuss how each of us needs someone who can see to guide us. Then blindfold two members of the family. Ask one of them to lead the other, while everyone looks on and, yes, laughs. Discuss again how we all need someone who can see to guide us. A blind guide is like having no guide at all.

>» Discuss it: The Bible is our guide. Often God uses people to guide us as well, but we must be careful to only follow those who know God, for all the others are blind.

Weed: Where in your day today did you see guides, or leaders, or teachers? Were those guides blind or seeing? Where in your day today were you a guide? Were you seeing or blind?

Friday
· · · · · ·

Till: God, you are alive! Through Jesus you show us how loving and wonderful you are. Help us to see you as you truly are and how much you love us.

Plant: Luke 7:1-17

Water:

» Act it: Act out verses 1-10. Who are you in the story? How does it feel to be that person?

» Act it: Act out verses 11-17. Who are you in the story? How does it feel to be that person?

» Discuss it: Jesus shows love by helping others. How can you show love today by helping others?

Weed: How did you show love today by helping others? How did someone love you by helping today? Thank God for that person.

Saturday
· · · · · · · · · ·

Till: Thank you, Jesus, for not only telling us that you are the Son of God, but for showing us that you are the Son of God. You didn't just say that you loved people; you showed that you loved people. You taught us that not only do words matter, but actions do too.

Plant: Luke 7:18-35

Water:

> » Discuss it: Many people can say that they follow God, but their words are only true if their actions follow God. In what ways do we say we follow God, but our actions are different? What can we do about it?

> » Race it: Run a three-legged race. Grab a few old neckties and invite the family outside. Have people pair up, standing side-by-side. Then tie their inside legs together so that each pair has three legs: the outside legs of each person, and the inside "leg" created by tying two legs together. Establish a starting and finish line, then race! After racing, discuss how each pair had to get their "three" legs working together to be able to win the race. Make the connection between actions and words: our words and our actions have to work together as well. We know that Jesus was the Son of God because his words and his actions worked together to show us the truth.

Weed: In what ways did your actions and words not work together today? Maybe you said you would do something, but you didn't. In what ways did your actions and words work together today? How did that feel?

EASTERTIDE, WEEK 5

······································

Sunday
·······

Till: God, you are the best Father there is! Thank you for listening to us and giving us good things.

Plant: Matthew 7:7-14

Water:

> » Ask it: What do you want people to do for you today? Now plan how you can do that for them.

> » Pray it: What do you need for today? Pray as a family for God to meet those needs today.

Weed: What made you happy or sad today? What did you do for others today? How did God meet your needs?

Monday
·······

Till: Help us, Lord Jesus, to live in your love. Remind us that you love us so much, it doesn't matter what others think of us.

Plant: Luke 7:36-50

Water:

>» Act it: Act out today's story. With which character do you have most in common? Why? What does the Holy Spirit have to say to you?

>» Think it: In the last two verses the people at the dinner table start talking about Jesus behind his back. They don't believe he is God's Son and can forgive sins. Are there people in your life who don't believe that God has made you and given you a special purpose? Do as Jesus did: ignore them.

Weed: Take some quiet time and confess to Jesus the sins you struggled with today. Accept his forgiveness and love like the woman did. Did you run into people who talked behind your back today? Were you able to ignore them? How did it feel?

Tuesday
. . . .

Till: Thank you, God, for good soil. Help us to know how to till, plant, water and weed our gardens. Please cause our gardens to grow!

Plant: Luke 8:1-15

Water:

>» Draw it: Take a piece of paper and divide it into four numbered sections. In Section 1 draw the part of the passage where we read about the "seed that fell on the road; it was trampled down and the birds ate it." In Section 2 draw the part where "seed fell in the gravel; it sprouted, but it didn't have any good roots and it withered." In Section 3 draw the part where "seed fell in the weeds, and the weeds grew up and strangled it." In Section 4 draw the part in which the "seed fell in rich dirt and produced a bumper crop."

» Discuss it: Reread verses 11-15, then look at the drawings and ask: Which section are you today? Where did the seed fall? How can we make the soil better?

Weed: When were you happy or sad today? When did you think about the parable today? How did the seed produce fruit? How can you make your soil better tomorrow?

Wednesday

Till: You are awesome, Jesus! You are the light of the world. Help us to understand with our bodies and our spirits that you have made us also to be lights. Help us to spread your light today.

Plant: Luke 8:16-25

Water:

» Act it: Act out verses 22-25. Who are you in the story? Why? What does Jesus have to say to you?

» Do it: Turn off all the lights. Take a flashlight and tape paper over the end so that the light barely shines through. Guide the family around the house with only the flashlight. See how long it takes for someone to ask why it's covered in paper, or suggests taking the paper off. Discuss that fact that Jesus made us the light of the world, and he wants to use us to bring the light of God into the lives of people. How brightly we shine matters.

» Ask it: How can you bring the light of God into your day, and into people who you will talk with today?

» Visit the Altar: Spend a few moments looking at the Christ candle. Think about God's light.

Weed: How did your light shine today? Where did you see the light of God in someone else?

Thursday

· · · · · · · · · ·

Till: Thank you, Jesus, for being the great healer. Show us how good it is to be healed. Show us how good it is to be changed. We want you to heal us and change us.

Plant: Luke 8:26-39

Water:

> » Act it: Act out the scene in today's story. Who are you? What does the Holy Spirit have to say to you about this scene?

> » Discuss it: Change can be difficult. We often like things just the way they are. But God wants to change us into being more loving, more kind: more like Jesus. What change do you think God is talking with you about? How can you work with God in this change?

Weed: What made you happy or sad today? How did you try to work with God in this change today?

Friday

· · · · · ·

Till: Jesus you are never late. You are always right on time. Help us to trust in your loving care.

Plant: Luke 8:40-56

Water:

> » Act it: If you have enough people, act out the whole scene. Then ask: who do you think had to have more faith, the woman who was bleeding or the father? Why? Who are you most like in the story?

> » List it: Faith is built on knowledge of God. There are lots of things we know about God. For example we know that he makes the sun to come up each day. We know that he makes the rain to fall to the earth and that he waters the plants. We know that he created us and loves us.

What else do you know about God? Make a family list, and post it so everyone can be reminded.

Weed: Where did you see the love and care of God in your day? How did it help you to know more about God? When did you need to have trust or faith in God today?

Saturday
....

Till: God, we are amazed that you like to work with us. You want to use children, and men and women. You made us to work with you. Help us to learn how to work like you work.

Plant: Luke 9:1-17

Water:

» Discuss it: Reread the passage, counting the number of times Jesus asks "the Twelve" to do something. He is teaching them to be the light of the world. He is teaching them to be his hands. In Matthew 5, Jesus says that he wants us also to be the light of the world; he wants to use us as his hands.

» Ask it: How can you be the hands of Jesus today?

Weed: How were you the hands of Jesus today? How was someone the hands of Jesus to you today?

EASTERTIDE, WEEK 6

Sunday

Till: God, your kingdom is on the move! It's expanding and growing, right here and right now, quietly among us. Help us to be on the lookout for your kingdom today.

Plant: Matthew 13:24-34

Water:

» Make it: If you can, make a loaf of bread with your kids today. Explain how the yeast, which looks like such a small part of the ingredients, causes the bread to rise. Or, if that's not practical, you could also show your kids a tiny seed and the large plant that comes from it.

» Enter it: Jesus tells these stories to explain that the rule of God is spreading, and growing, right among us, even though it may not look like much right now. What are some ways you have seen God's will being done among us recently? Keep your eyes out for the Kingdom today.

Weed: What did you enjoy about today? Where did you see God's kingdom among us today? When did you have an opportunity to help his will be done?

Monday

Till: Jesus, your ways aren't like ours. When you lead, you serve. When you conquer, you lay down your life. When you save us, you lose yourself. We aren't used to this, and we need you to help us understand.

Plant: Plant: Luke 9:8–27

Water:

> » Imagine it: How do you think the disciples felt when Peter said Jesus was the Messiah (the Chosen One who would save Israel from their enemies)? How would you expect someone to save a nation from its enemies? Now, how do you think they felt when Jesus said that he would suffer, be found guilty, and be killed?

> » Apply it: Jesus knows that God's way is an upside-down way. With God's way the most effective way to be strong is to become a servant and yield our way to help others. Why is this hard? How could you live "upside-down" today?

Weed: What made you happy or sad today? Where did you get to live "upside-down"? When was a time when you could have served, but chose not to?

Tuesday

Till: Father, against all our expectations, you really want to give us what we need, and you want us to ask for it! Give us what we need today: food, and love, and forgiveness, and your presence above all else.

Plant: Luke 11:1-13

Water:

> » Enter it: When Jesus' disciples ask him to teach them to pray, he doesn't give them a list of complicated, detached petitions. Instead, he teaches

them to pray directly for their everyday, usual needs. What are some everyday needs that God would want you to ask for?

» Draw it: Draw some of the things that you can ask God to help you with. Post the drawing as a reminder where you'll see it. When you pass by the picture today, pause and ask God to help with one of the things you've drawn.

Weed: What made you feel good today? How did it feel to ask God to help with what you need? How did God meet your needs?

Wednesday

Till: Invite the family to sit quiet for a moment, and enter this prayer practice together:

Jesus, you are with us. (Take a deep breath and relax!)

Jesus, you are with us. (Another deep breath!)

Jesus, you are with us. (Smile!)

Plant: Luke 12:22-31

Water:

» Enter it: Go outside and find something lovely that God has made—a flower, a pinecone, a rock—and bring it inside. (This means you probably shouldn't pick something alive, unless it's the cat!) Have a show-and-tell of how God provides abundantly.

» Apply it: What is something you have been worried about recently? How would your feelings change if you could see God's goodness? How can you see God's goodness today?

Weed: Where did you see God's goodness and love today? How did that affect your level of worry or fear?

Ascension Day (Thursday)

Till: Jesus, you have died, you have risen, you have ascended into heaven and you are seated at the right hand of the Father! You are on the throne, in charge, right now! We praise you!

Plant: Matt. 28:16-20

Water:

> » Act it: Read the passage in Acts 1:1-11, and have kids act it out. Have one of the lighter-weight kids play Jesus, and make the child "disappear into the clouds" by putting him or her on your shoulders, or carrying the kid away! Have fun!

> » Enter it: Today is 40 days after Easter, and that's how long Jesus was with his disciples after he rose again. Then he was taken up into heaven to be with his Father. But before he went, Jesus gave his disciples one last instruction: train people in my way! Name some ways you are being trained in Jesus' way.

Weed: What made you feel good or bad today? When did you let yourself be trained in Jesus' way today? When did you avoid Jesus' way?

Friday

Till: Jesus, you are the Son, the Chosen One of the Father! We will listen to you!

Plant: Luke 9:28-36

Water:

> » Act it: Have kids act this scene out—you could wrap "Jesus" in a white sheet when he transfigures.

> » Apply it: When Jesus was revealed in his glory, Peter, John and James got to see how amazing he really is, even though most of the time had

Jesus hidden the fullness of his power. God told them to listen to Jesus. How can you listen to Jesus today?

Weed: When did you listen for Jesus today? Do you think you heard him? How does Jesus' voice sound to you? (Parents: Children often have an easier time hearing God than we do, because they are more ready to listen. But kids, like young Samuel, need help learning to know when God is speaking. You can help them train their ears. For example, if they report that Jesus sounds "angry" or "mean" or "disappointed," they need help to understand that's not how Jesus speaks. Gentle instruction can go a long way here. Reread the "Family Listening" section in the Series Introduction.)

Saturday

Till: God, we need your help. We don't have a good sense of your greatness; we don't see the world in your light. Help us grow to understand and see the world like you do.

Plant: Luke 9:37-50

Water:

> » Enter it: In these three little stories the disciples are first unable to save a boy from a demon, then not able to understand that Jesus would be betrayed, and then they argue about who is most important. These stories show us how hard it is for us people to understand God's ways. Have you ever felt that you don't understand God's ways?

> » Apply it: A few days ago we read about Jesus' teaching the disciples to pray, asking for what they need. Today ask God to help you understand him better.

> » Visit the Altar: Draw a picture in the sand of what you need today.

Weed: When today did you ask God to help you understand him better? How did it feel to ask for his help?

EASTERTIDE, WEEK 7

Sunday

Till: Jesus, give us courage and hope when people treat us badly because we trust you. Help us trust that you are standing up for us and will give us all the help we need.

Plant: Matt. 10:24-33, 40-42

Water:

» Enter it: Have you ever had anyone treat you badly because you wouldn't disobey God, or because you love Him? Tell about a time you were made fun of for being good.

» Draw it: Jesus says that he is cheering for us before God in heaven. Draw a picture that helps you remember that truth, and put it someplace you'll see it today.

Weed: How did it feel to know that Jesus was standing up for you today? When did you feel alone today? How can you remember that Jesus is with you and is cheering for you?

Monday

Till: Jesus, help us to follow you no matter what. On those days we hurt and we have bad days, help us to keep on following you, through thick and thin. Help us to trust that your way is best.

Plant: Luke 9:51-62

Water:

> » Act it: Have kids play the part of the three people who offer to follow Jesus. Use your imagination: How do they respond to Jesus' replies?

> » Enter it: What are some ways you tend to ask Jesus to work? What does the work of Jesus in your life look like right now? What is God up to?

Weed: Where did you look for what God was up to today? Were you able to jump into God's Kingdom life today? Why or why not?

Tuesday

Till: God, you send us out to proclaim your Kingdom, just as Jesus proclaimed your Kingdom. While not everyone wants to hear it, we always proclaim by loving others. Help us proclaim your kingdom through love today.

Plant: Luke 10:1-16

Water:

> » Enter it: Jesus tells his disciples to go out, ready to tell people about how God is close and life with him is available now. He adds that not everyone is going to want to hear it, and his disciples shouldn't be surprised by that. Why do you think people might not want to hear? What do you think makes people want God's kingdom?

> » Apply it: What are some ways you could show people today that God's kingdom is right on their doorstep? How can you say it with words, and without words?

Weed: Did you get to show anyone God's kingdom today? How did it feel? What made you feel happy or sad today?

Wednesday

Till: God, your kingdom is right here among us, so that even the simplest of us can get to it. Children and newcomers and sinners belong in God's kingdom! Hallelujah, you are close!

Plant: Luke 10:17-24

Water:

» Draw it: Jesus rejoices that God's kingdom is wide open. Even if smart, powerful people refuse to enter, that doesn't mean it's far away or hard to find. Anyone who really wants to find it, can. Create a picture that shows God's kingdom open to everybody who wants to find it. What surprising people find their way in?

» Enter it: Jesus also says that the great prize of the kingdom isn't what we think it is. It's not big displays of power, but the quiet, constant presence of God with us forever. How can you practice being with God today?

Weed: How did you practice being with God today? How does it feel when you know that God is with you?

Thursday

Till: Jesus, you came among us to become our neighbor. You moved right on into our space and loved us. Help us to find ways to be a good neighbor to those around us today.

Plant: Luke 10:25-37

Water:

> » Act it: Have children act out today's parable.

> » Apply it: In response to the lawyer's question, "Who is my neighbor," Jesus tells a story that changes the question entirely. The important question is, "Who can I become a neighbor to?" How could you be a good neighbor to people around you today?

> » Visit the Altar: Draw a picture in the sand of your neighbor. Pray for that person.

Weed: Who were you a good neighbor to today? How did it feel to be a good neighbor?

Friday
......

Till: Jesus, you are the one thing that matters. Life with you is real life. We get so busy and distracted. Help us to return to you!

Plant: Luke 10:38-42

Water:

> » Draw it: Draw a picture of Mary and Martha in this story. How do you think Mary feels as she sits at Jesus' feet? How do you think Martha feels as she is busy in the kitchen?

> » Apply it: Jesus isn't saying we should never do chores. Instead, we can learn not to be distracted by our work, and keep our focus on Jesus in the midst of our tasks. What is one chore you could do with Jesus today? Try it!

Weed: How did it feel to do chores with Jesus? Was it hard or easy to remember to work with him? What can you do with Jesus tomorrow?

Saturday

Till: Jesus, you are our strong Commander in Chief in the battle against evil. You are mighty, powerful, and you will triumph!

Plant: Luke 11:14-23

Water:

> »   Draw it: God has an enemy. His enemy is anyone or anything that hurts his children. His enemy is hate and greed and pride. He will not stop until his enemy is destroyed. Draw a picture of God destroying the things that hurt his children.

> »   Discuss it: Evil and pain are real forces in the world. Children are often victims of evil and pain. Invite your children into a discussion about evil, about where they have seen it or experienced it. Afterwards, be sure to thank and praise Jesus for being the triumphant destroyer of evil.

Weed: What made you happy or sad today? When today did you see or help good to triumph over evil?

WEEK OF PENTECOST

Normally, Pentecost is not a season unto itself. In fact the Holy Spirit gets one day in the traditional calendar. We've decided to alter this a bit and draw Pentecost out for the whole week. Seems fitting, doesn't it? We thought so too.

The color for this one wonderful week of celebrating the coming of the Holy Spirit is red, a lovely fiery red that reminds us of the all-consuming energy of God that both protects us and inspires our awe. Wind is also a big theme this week. Wind is a magnificent visual for the Holy Spirit. We can see the effects of the wind, but we cannot see the wind. Take the time to sit outside with your people in the wind, talking about the wind. Talk about how God is always working to help us know more about him, and he loves to use his creation to do it.

Seasonal Fun:

» Make a pinwheel: or better yet, buy one! However, if you can't find one to buy:

  » Cut a 4" x 4" square out of a piece of paper.

  » Take your square piece of paper and fold it in half. You'll then have a triangle.

  » Fold the paper triangle in half.

  » Unfold the paper. Leaving a 1-1/2" square in the middle, cut the paper up the folds.

> » Fold 1/3 of each triangle over. You may want to use tape to reinforce the fold so your pinwheel doesn't break apart.

> » Get a straight pin and pencil. Put a pin through the middle of the paper pin wheel and stick it into the eraser head of the pencil. Your pinwheel is ready!

» Fly a kite in the wind! Imagine the wind of the Spirit blowing among the believers

» Have a bonfire, if it's not a windy day. Fire is the representation of the presence of God in many stories in the Bible. Gather the kids and neighbors around the fire, roast some marshmallows, and tell the story of Pentecost.

» Add more candles (battery powered ones are good, too!) to the Family Altar, as many as you can.

A Pentecost Skit

» Materials: paper, markers, tongue depressors, red streamers, glue

» Divide the family into two groups: actors and narrators.

» Say: We're going to have a reenactment of Pentecost, the day God sent the Holy Spirit. We need actors who are Jesus' friends, actors who are the fire (or the Spirit), and narrators.

» Props: Invite the family to design and create paper fire attached to the tongue depressors

» Actors: If you have children who can read, invite them to be the narrators; if not, one adult can be the sole narrator while everyone else is an actor. The actors must listen to know what to do.

Begin with an empty stage. (A stage can be made on bare floor, by taping off a rectangle.)

> Narrator 1: Jesus died, came back to life, spent some time with his friends and then went to get things ready with God. Just before Jesus

left, he told his friends God was sending someone else. Someone to help, and comfort them; someone who would never leave them.

Narrator 2: But today Jesus' friends are all hiding out in a room. The Romans killed Jesus, and his friends are worried they might be next. (The actors who are being his friends rush onto the stage, and pretend to close a door behind them. They look nervous and afraid.)

Narrator 1: Suddenly a noise came from heaven. It sounded like strong wind blowing. It sounded like a tornado! (The friends hold their ears and look even more afraid.)

Narrator 2: Then they saw something that looked like flames of fire on each of the friends' heads. (Actors who are being the fire enter the stage and hold the fire above the heads of the friends.)

Narrator 1: They were filled with the Holy Spirit and they began to speak different languages. The Holy Spirit was giving them power. They were not afraid.

Trade groups, and do the skit again.

Discuss: The Holy Spirit comforts and guides us. He can help us not to be afraid, and help us know what to do. He is with us all the time. We can talk to him. If we listen very quietly, we can hear him tell us that God loves us. Today we made a reminder of the fire that the people saw on Pentecost. It is our reminder to sit quietly each day and listen to the Holy Spirit.

Invite the children to think about some times that would be good to be quiet to listen to the Holy Spirit: before bed, right when they wake up, in the car. Encourage the children to put the prop "fire" from the skit in a place that can remind them to listen (perhaps by their bed, or on their wall where they can see it when they wake up).

Pentecost Sunday

Till: Holy Spirit, you have come and you lead us to God! Thank you for helping us know Jesus and walk with him today. We praise you!

Plant: John 14:21-29

Water:

> » Draw it: Read the passage from Acts 2 and draw your favorite part of this story.

> » Pray it: Jesus says the Holy Spirit will make everything plain, which is the way we need it. What do you need the Holy Spirit to make plain today? Make your need into a prayer.

Weed: How did it feel to ask the Holy Spirit to help you today? When did you see the Holy Spirit teaching or guiding you today?

Pentecost Monday

Till: Jesus, you wash us from the inside out by sending the Holy Spirit! Cleanse our hearts today from everything bad, and fill us with your life!

Plant: Matthew 3:1-11

Water:

> » Enter it: John the Baptizer taught that Jesus wouldn't just clean the outside of us, but our hearts—he plans to change us from the inside! Is there a habit you have that you need help being cleansed of?

> » Pray it: Turn this into a short prayer: "Spirit, clean up my heart from..." or, "Jesus, wash away my..." You might write it on a 3x5 card, or choose an object that symbolizes your prayer, and carry it with you today. When you find yourself turning to that habit, or realize you already did, you could put your hand in your pocket, touch the object and say your personal prayer.

Weed: How did it feel to ask the Spirit to change you today? Did you notice yourself wanting or able to behave differently?

Pentecost Tuesday

Till: God, you know what we need, even before we ask—and you love giving! Thank you that we can be sure that when we ask for what we need, you will always provide it in just the right way.

Plant: Luke 11:3–13

Water:

» Imagine it: Jesus invites us to use our imagination with today's story. So go ahead—read the story again, using your imagination and all your senses. What would it be like to knock on someone's door late at night, in the cold air? Or, imagine being the cranky friend woken from sleep.

» Enter it: Jesus is telling us that God will be generous to give us his Spirit to help us, because He is the best Father you can imagine. Today, let's practice asking for the Spirit. Carry a key in your pocket (parents, if you have extra old keys that can be lost, you could give these to the kids. Or, you could make keys out of construction paper). That reminds us that we have the key to God's heart—the door is open, just ask! When you feel in need today, ask for God's Spirit, and see what happens.

» Visit the Altar: Draw in the sand something you need today.

Weed: When did you ask for the Spirit today? What happened? How did you feel?

Pentecost Wednesday

Till: Holy Spirit, we can't see you or touch you, but we want to experience you in our lives. Help us to recognize when you blow like wind through our hearts!

Plant: John 3:1-18, 34

Water:

» Play it: Jesus says the Spirit is like the wind—we don't see it, but we can tell when it's blowing because of what happens (leaves stirring in trees, our hair whipping around, kites sailing in the sky). Today, take some time to play in the wind: use your pinwheel, or fly a kite, or just run around where it's windy. (If today happens to be a still day, you could set up a fan in your house and leave it blowing as a reminder.)

» Apply it: Today, be on the lookout for the Holy Spirit. You might notice him if you get the idea to do something nice for someone. Or you might see him helping you not to do something you know is wrong. Or maybe you'll feel joy and peace and love for other people or for God—there he is! When you notice him, just say, "I see you, Spirit!"

Weed: Where did you see the Spirit today? What was it like to be on the lookout for him?

Pentecost Thursday

Till: God, when we live with you, our life flows like a river—your Spirit makes good things just pour on out of us to other people! Help us to live in your flow today!

Plant: John 7:37–46

Water:

» Play it: Today, Jesus tells us what life with him is like—when we trust Jesus, we discover that everything we need just flows on out of our hearts, because we have the Holy Spirit in us. He is there comforting, directing, helping, providing. And so life just flows—instead of working hard to grind out the right action, it just flows. Take some time today, if possible, to visit a river or a creek, a waterfall or a canal, and watch the water flow by. (Maybe float a paper boat just for fun.) While you're there, notice how the water isn't trying to flow. If you can't go today, you could plan a time soon.

» Apply it: In his book, *The Me I Want to Be*, John Ortberg suggests that we live in the Spirit in a simple way: "try softer." Just like a flowing stream of water, life with God means we don't grind our teeth and crank, we trust and surrender and rest in God's goodness and let the fruit grow. Today, when anything seems hard, scary, or like you need to try harder, take a 5-second pause, ask the Spirit to let life flow, and then try "softer" by imagining God helping you with your task. (This goes for homework as well as being nice!!!)

Weed: What was it like to "try softer?" Did you notice a difference? Where would you like to "try softer" tomorrow?

Pentecost Friday

Till: Holy Spirit, you show us the truth—thank you! We'd be lost without your help, because we don't know up from down or right from wrong on our own. Guide us into truth today, please!

Plant: John 15:26-27, 16:4–15

Water:

» **Play it:** Illustrate the Holy Spirit guiding us with a simple game. Blindfold a child, and let another be the guide through the house, telling them when to stop, when to turn, etc. Let everyone take a turn being guided. (If you suspect this might all end in tears, you might want to hover close, or perhaps the adult can be the guide for each child—whatever your people need!) Discuss how this is different from the "blind leading the blind"—the Holy Spirit knows where we are going!

> » **Apply it:** Today, practice asking the Holy Spirit for guidance. When you don't know what to do, or you don't know what is right, take a moment to pause and ask to be guided. As you move forward, imagine God at your side, just like in the game.

Weed: When did you ask for guidance today? How did that feel? Where do you need to ask for guidance and help tomorrow?

Pentecost Saturday

Till: Jesus, you have breathed your Holy Spirit into us, the breath of life! Help us to breathe in your presence and breathe out our fear.

Plant: John 20:19–23

Water:

> » Play it: Take some time to practice "Breathe In, Breathe Out." For a few moments, be still and focus on your breath. Every time you breathe in, imagine God's love and presence filling you up. When you breathe out, imagine your fear and loneliness going away. You might take a few opportunities throughout today to do this (driving in the car, a moment before mealtime, as you're lying down for a nap.)

> » Enter it: Where do you need God with you today? What fears or worries do you need to let go of?

Weed: What was it like playing "Breathe in, Breathe out"? Did it help you? Was there a time you forgot and held onto your fears? How could you remember to release them to God tomorrow?

CHURCH YEAR CALENDAR

Year	Advent	Lent	Holy Week	Easter	Pentecost
2013-14	Dec 1	March 5	April 13	April 20	June 8
2014-15	Nov 30	Feb 18	March 29	April 5	May 24
2015-16	Nov 29	Feb 10	March 20	March 27	May 15
2016-17	Nov 27	March 1	April 9	April 16	June 4
2017-18	Dec 3	Feb 14	March 25	April 1	May 20
2018-19	Dec 2	March 6	April 14	April 21	June 9
2019-20	Dec 1	Feb 26	April 5	April 12	May 31
2020-21	Nov 29	Feb 17	March 28	April 4	May 23
2021-22	Nov 28	March 2	April 10	April 17	June 5
2022-23	Nov 27	Feb 22	April 2	April 9	May 28
2023-24	Dec 3	Feb 14	March 24	March 31	May 19
2024-25	Dec 1	March 5	April 13	April 20	June 8
2025-26	Nov 30	Feb 18	March 29	April 5	May 24
2026-27	Nov 29	Feb 10	March 21	March 28	May 16
2027-28	Nov 28	March 1	April 9	April 16	June 4
2028-29	Dec 3	Feb 14	March 25	April 1	May 27

CONTRIBUTORS

Lacy Finn Borgo

Lacy Finn Borgo writes for the spiritual formation of children because she has children and she likes them. She has a Master's Degree in Education from the State University of New York Geneseo and has taught in both public and private schools in Texas, New York, Colorado, and Kazakhstan. Lacy is a graduate of the Renovaré Institute for Spiritual Formation. She is the author of *Life with God for Children: Engaging Biblical Stories and Practices for Spiritual Formation* released by Renovaré. Lacy has written three picture books—*Big Mama's Baby, Day and Night,* and *The Mighty Hurricane.* Lacy lives in Colorado where she tends both the physical and spiritual gardens of her family.

Ben Barczi

Ben Barczi serves as Pastor of Spiritual Formation at First Baptist Church in San Luis Obispo, California. He is a graduate of California Polytechnic in San Luis Obispo, where he studied Philosophy, and a graduate of the Renovaré Institute for Spiritual Formation. Ben loves teaching about spiritual formation, and enjoys living a semi-monastic life ordered by the rhythms of Daily Prayer, regular solitude, and good conversations at amazing local coffeeshops.

Made in the USA
Middletown, DE
25 February 2019